THE YALE SHAKESPEARE

EDITED BY

WILBUR L. CROSS   TUCKER BROOKE

ALL'S WELL THAT ENDS WELL

EDITED BY

ARTHUR E. CASE

NEW HAVEN AND LONDON

YALE UNIVERSITY PRESS

CONTENTS

The facsimile opposite reproduces the title-page of the Elizabethan Club copy of the first separate edition of 'All's Well that Ends Well.' Tonson 'and the rest of the Proprietors' claimed a perpetual copyright in Shakespeare's plays as successors to the publishers of the first Folio.

ALL's WELL

THAT

ENDS WELL.

A

COMEDY.

By Mr. *WILLIAM SHAKESPEAR.*

LONDON:

Printed for J. TONSON, and the reſt of the PRO-
PRIETORS; and ſold by the Bookſellers of
London and *Weſtminſter.*

DCCXXXIV.

[DRAMATIS PERSONÆ.

KING OF FRANCE
DUKE OF FLORENCE
BERTRAM, *Count of Rousillon*
LAFEU, *an old Lord*
PAROLLES, *a parasitical follower of Bertram*
Several young French Lords, that serve with Bertram
    in the Florentine wars
RINALDO, *a Steward,* } *Servants to the Countess of*
LAVACHE, *a Clown,* }   *Rousillon*

COUNTESS OF ROUSILLON, *Mother to Bertram*
HELENA, *daughter to* Gerard de Narbon, *a famous*
    physician, some time since dead
An old Widow of Florence
DIANA, *daughter to the Widow*
VIOLENTA, }
MARIANA, } *Neighbors and friends to the Widow*
Lords attending on the King, Officers, Soldiers, etc.

SCENE: *partly in France and partly in Tuscany.*]

Dramatis Personæ first given by Rowe, ed. 1709.

All's Well that Ends Well

ACT FIRST

Scene One

[Rousillon.   A Room in the Countess's Palace]

*Enter young Bertram, Count of Rousillon, his Mother
[the Countess], and Helena, [and] Lord Lafeu,
all in black.*

Count. In delivering my son from me, I bury
a second husband.

Ber. And I, in going, madam, weep o'er my
father's death anew; but I must attend his 4
majesty's command, to whom I am now in
ward, evermore in subjection.

Laf. You shall find of the king a husband,
madam; you, sir, a father. He that so generally 8
is at all times good must of necessity hold his
virtue to you, whose worthiness would stir it up
where it wanted rather than lack it where there
is such abundance.   12

Count. What hope is there of his majesty's
amendment?

Laf. He hath abandoned his physicians,
madam, under whose practices he hath per- 16
secuted time with hope, and finds no other
advantage in the process but only the losing of
hope by time.

Count. This young gentlewoman had a fa- 20

4 attend: *pay heed to*
5 to . . . ward: *under whose guardianship I now am*
8 generally: *universally*   9 hold: *continue to display*
14 amendment: *improvement in health*
16, 17 persecuted . . . hope: *spent much time in hoping*

ther,—O, that 'had!' how sad a passage 'tis!—
whose skill was almost as great as his honesty;
had it stretched so far, would have made nature immortal, and death should have play for 24
lack of work. Would, for the king's sake, he
were living! I think it would be the death of
the king's disease.

Laf. How called you the man you speak of, 28
madam?

Count. He was famous, sir, in his profession,
and it was his great right to be so: Gerard de
Narbon.   32

Laf. He was excellent indeed, madam: the
king very lately spoke of him admiringly and
mourningly. He was skilful enough to have
lived still, if knowledge could be set up against 36
mortality.

Ber. What is it, my good lord, the king
languishes of?

Laf. A fistula, my lord.   40

Ber. I heard not of it before.

Laf. I would it were not notorious. Was
this gentlewoman the daughter of Gerard de
Narbon?   44

Count. His sole child, my lord; and bequeathed to my overlooking. I have those hopes
of her good that her education promises: her
dispositions she inherits, which makes fair gifts 48
fairer; for where an unclean mind carries virtuous qualities, there commendations go with
pity; they are virtues and traitors too: in her

---

21 passage: *expression*   31 his great right: *clearly his due*
36 set up against: *opposed to*   40 fistula: *a sinuous ulcer*
46 overlooking: *supervision*   48 dispositions: *natural inclinations*
49 virtuous qualities: *admirable intellectual qualities*
50 go with pity: *are given with regret*

they are the better for their simpleness; she de- 52
rives her honesty and achieves her goodness.

Laf. Your commendations, madam, get from
her tears.

Count. 'Tis the best brine a maiden can sea- 56
son her praise in.   The remembrance of her
father never approaches her heart but the
tyranny of her sorrows takes all livelihood from
her cheek.   No more of this, Helena; go to, no 60
more, lest it be rather thought you affect a
sorrow, than to have—

Hel. I do affect a sorrow indeed, but I have
it too.   64

Laf. Moderate lamentation is the right of
the dead, excessive grief the enemy to the living.

Count. If the living be enemy to the grief, the
excess makes it soon mortal.   68

Ber. Madam, I desire your holy wishes.

Laf. How understand we that?

Count. Be thou blest, Bertram; and succeed thy
    father
In manners, as in shape! thy blood and virtue   72
Contend for empire in thee, and thy goodness
Share with thy birthright!   Love all, trust a few,
Do wrong to none: be able for thine enemy
Rather in power than use, and keep thy friend   76
Under thy own life's key: be check'd for silence,
But never tax'd for speech.   What heaven more will
That thee may furnish, and my prayers pluck down,
Fall on thy head! [*To Lafeu.*] Farewell, my lord;   80

52 simpleness: *lack of complexity*   59 livelihood: *liveliness*
63, 64 *Cf. n.*   67, 68 *Cf. n.*   70 *Cf. n.*   72 thy: *may thy*
74 Share . . . birthright: *equal your inherited nobility*
75, 76 be . . . use: *be able to conquer your enemy, but spare him*
76, 77 keep . . . key: *protect your friend with your life*
77 check'd: *reproached*   78 tax'd: *rebuked*   will: *may desire*
79 That .. . furnish: *that may adorn your character*

'Tis an unseason'd courtier; good my lord,
Advise him.

 Laf.   He cannot want the best
That shall attend his love.

 Count. Heaven bless him! Farewell, Bertram. 84
              [*Exit.*]

 Ber. [*To Helena.*] The best wishes that can
be forged in your thoughts be servants to you!
Be comfortable to my mother, your mistress,
and make much of her.   88

 Laf. Farewell, pretty lady: you must hold
the credit of your father.

        [*Exeunt Bertram and Lafeu.*]

 Hel. O, were that all! I think not on my father,
And these great tears grace his remembrance more 92
Than those I shed for him. What was he like?
I have forgot him: my imagination
Carries no favour in 't but Bertram's.
I am undone: there is no living, none,   96
If Bertram be away. 'Twere all one
That I should love a bright particular star
And think to wed it, he is so above me:
In his bright radiance and collateral light   100
Must I be comforted, not in his sphere.
Th' ambition in my love thus plagues itself:
The hind that would be mated by the lion
Must die for love. 'Twas pretty, though a plague, 104
To see him every hour; to sit and draw
His arched brows, his hawking eye, his curls,
In our heart's table; heart too capable

82, 83 He . . . love; *cf. n.*   85, 86 *Cf. n.*
87 Be comfortable to: *console*
89 hold the credit: *uphold the good name*
92, 93: And . . . him; *cf. n.*   95 favour: *face*
97, 98 'Twere . . . should: *I might as well* 98 particular: *individual*
100, 101 *Cf. n.*   106 hawking: *hawk-like*
107 table: *tablet* capable: *ready to receive the impress*

Of every line and trick of his sweet favour: 108
But now he's gone, and my idolatrous fancy
Must sanctify his relics.   Who comes here?

Enter Parolles.

One that goes with him: I love him for his sake;
And yet I know him a notorious liar,   112
Think him a great way fool, solely a coward;
Yet these fix'd evils sit so fit in him,
That they take place, when virtue's steely bones
Looks bleak i' th' cold wind: withal, full oft we see 116
Cold wisdom waiting on superfluous folly.

    Par. Save you, fair queen!

    Hel. And you, monarch!

    Par. No.   120

    Hel. And no.

    Par. Are you meditating on virginity?

    Hel. Ay.   You have some stain of soldier in
you; let me ask you a question.   Man is enemy 124
to virginity; how may we barricado it against
him?

    Par. Keep him out.

    Hel. But he assails; and our virginity, though 128
valiant in the defence, yet is weak.   Unfold to
us some warlike resistance.

    Par. There is none: man, setting down before
you, will undermine you and blow you up.   132

    Hel. Bless our poor virginity from under-
miners and blowers up!   Is there no military
policy, how virgins might blow up men?

108 trick: *peculiarity*   110 sanctify his relics: *worship his memory*
113 a great way: *largely*   solely: *altogether*
114 sit . . . him: *become him so well*
115 take place: *find acceptance*   steely: *unbending*
116 Looks; *cf. n.*   withal: *therewith*   117 superfluous: *luxurious*
120, 121 *Cf. n.*   123 stain: *trace*
131 setting down: *setting down his batteries*

Par. Virginity being blown down, man will 136
quicklier be blown up: marry, in blowing him
down again, with the breach yourselves made,
you lose your city. It is not politic in the com-
monwealth of nature to preserve virginity. Loss 140
of virginity is rational increase, and there was
never virgin got till virginity was first lost.
That you were made of is metal to make virgins.
Virginity, by being once lost, may be ten times 144
found: by being ever kept, it is ever lost. 'Tis
too cold a companion: away with 't!

Hel. I will stand for 't a little, though therefore I die a virgin.   148

Par. There's little can be said in 't; 'tis
against the rule of nature. To speak on the part
of virginity is to accuse your mothers, which
is most infallible disobedience. He that hangs 152
himself is a virgin: virginity murders itself, and
should be buried in highways, out of all sanctified limit, as a desperate offendress against nature. Virginity breeds mites, much like a cheese, 156
consumes itself to the very paring, and so dies
with feeding his own stomach. Besides, virginity
is peevish, proud, idle, made of self-love, which
is the most inhibited sin in the canon. Keep it 160
not; you cannot choose but lose by 't! Out with 't!
within the year it will make itself two, which is
a goodly increase, and the principal itself not
much the worse. Away with 't!   164

Hel. How might one do, sir, to lose it to her
own liking?

137 marry: *by the Virgin Mary*
143 metal: *material*
149 in 't: *for it*
154, 155 sanctified limit; *cf. n.*
160 inhibited: *forbidden*

141 rational: *reasonable*
147 stand: *fight*
152 infallible: *unquestionable*
158 his; *cf. n.*
161 Out with 't: *put it to use*

Par. Let me see: marry, ill, to like him that
ne'er it likes. 'Tis a commodity will lose 168
the gloss with lying; the longer kept, the less
worth: off with 't, while 'tis vendible; answer the
time of request. Virginity, like an old courtier,
wears her cap out of fashion; richly suited, but 172
unsuitable: just like the brooch and the tooth-
pick, which wear not now. Your date is better in
your pie and your porridge than in your cheek:
and your virginity, your old virginity, is like one 176
of our French withered pears; it looks ill, it eats
drily; marry, 'tis a withered pear; it was formerly better; marry, yet 'tis a withered pear.
Will you anything with it?   180
Hel. Not my virginity yet.

There shall your master have a thousand loves,
A mother, and a mistress, and a friend,
A phœnix, captain, and an enemy,   184
A guide, a goddess, and a sovereign,
A counsellor, a traitress, and a dear,
His humble ambition, proud humility,
His jarring concord, and his discord dulcet,   188
His faith, his sweet disaster; with a world
Of pretty, fond, adoptious christendoms,
That blinking Cupid gossips. Now shall he—
I know not what he shall. God send him well!   192
The court's a learning-place, and he is one—
  Par. What one, i' faith?
  Hel. That I wish well. 'Tis pity—
  Par. What's pity?   196

167, 168 that . . . likes: *whom it does not please*
169 lying: *lying unused*
170 answer . . . request: *meet the demand*   172 suited: *dressed*
174 wear not: *are not in fashion*   date: *used punningly*
181 Not: *not with*   182-191 *Cf. n.*
188 dulcet: *sweet*   190 adoptious christendoms: *nicknames*
191 blinking: *blind*   gossips: *is sponsor for*

Hel. That wishing well had not a body in 't,
Which might be felt; that we, the poorer born,
Whose baser stars do shut us up in wishes,
Might with effects of them follow our friends,   200
And show what we alone must think, which never
Returns us thanks.

Enter [a] Page.

Page. Monsieur Parolles, my lord calls for
you.   [*Exit.*] 204

Par. Little Helen, farewell: if I can remember thee, I will think of thee at court.

Hel. Monsieur Parolles, you were born under
a charitable star.   208

Par. Under Mars, I.

Hel. I especially think, under Mars.

Par. Why under Mars?

Hel. The wars hath so kept you under that 212
you must needs be born under Mars.

Par. When he was predominant.

Hel. When he was retrograde, I think rather.

Par. Why think you so?   216

Hel. You go so much backward when you
fight.

Par. That's for advantage.

Hel. So is running away, when fear proposes 220
the safety: but the composition that your valour
and fear makes in you is a virtue of a good wing,
and I like the wear well.

Par. I am so full of businesses I cannot 224
answer thee acutely. I will return perfect cour-

199 *Whose less exalted destinies confine us to wishing merely*
200 effects: *execution*   201 alone must: *can only*
214, 215 *Cf. n.*   219 for advantage: *for strategic purposes*
221 composition: *compromise*   222 virtue . . . wing; *cf. n.*
223 wear: *fashion*

tier; in the which, my instruction shall serve to
naturalize thee, so thou wilt be capable of a
courtier's counsel, and understand what advice 228
shall thrust upon thee; else thou diest in thine
unthankfulness, and thine ignorance makes thee
away: farewell.   When thou hast leisure, say thy
prayers; when thou hast none, remember thy 232
friends.   Get thee a good husband, and use him
as he uses thee: so, farewell.   [*Exit.*]

   Hel. Our remedies oft in ourselves do lie,
Which we ascribe to heaven: the fated sky   236
Gives us free scope; only doth backward pull
Our slow designs when we ourselves are dull.
What power is it which mounts my love so high,
That makes me see, and cannot feed mine eye?   240
The mightiest space in fortune nature brings
To join like likes, and kiss like native things.
Impossible be strange attempts to those
That weigh their pains in sense, and do suppose   244
What hath been cannot be: who ever strove
To show her merit, that did miss her love?
The king's disease—my project may deceive me,
But my intents are fix'd and will not leave me.   248
                                                  Exit.

226 in the which: *in which (court etiquette)*
227 naturalize: *familiarize*   capable of: *able to comprehend*
230, 231 makes thee away: *will destroy you*
231-233 When . . . friends; *cf. n.*   236 fated sky: *destiny*
239 mounts . . . high: *fixes my love on so high an object*
241, 242 *Cf. n.*   243 strange attempts: *unusual undertakings*
244 weigh . . . sense: *estimate their labor by reason*
246 miss: *fail to attain*   247 deceive: *disappoint*

Scene Two

[*Paris.   A Room in the King's Palace.*]

Flourish [*of*] *Cornets.   Enter the King of France,
with letters, and divers Attendants.*

King. The Florentines and Senoys are by th' ears;
Have fought with equal fortune, and continue
A braving war.

    1. Lord.   So 'tis reported, sir.

    King. Nay, 'tis most credible: we here receive it   **4**
A certainty, vouch'd from our cousin Austria,
With caution that the Florentine will move us
For speedy aid; wherein our dearest friend
Prejudicates the business, and would seem   **8**
To have us make denial.

    1. Lord.   His love and wisdom,
Approv'd so to your majesty, may plead
For amplest credence.

    King.   He hath arm'd our answer,
And Florence is denied before he comes: **12**
Yet, for our gentlemen that mean to see
The Tuscan service, freely have they leave
To stand on either part.

    2. Lord.   It well may serve
A nursery to our gentry, who are sick   **16**
For breathing and exploit.

    King.   What's he comes here?

1 Senoys: *Siennese, dwellers in Sienna*   by th' ears: *in combat*
3 braving: *defiant*   1. Lord: *cf. n.*
4, 5 receive . . . certainty: *are made certain of it*
5 cousin Austria: *fellow ruler of Austria*   6 move: *petition*
8 Prejudicates the business: *gives his opinion of the matter in advance*
8, 9 would . . . us: *seems to wish us to*
10 Approv'd so: *so often proved*
11 arm'd: *strengthened*   12 Florence: *the Duke of Florence*
15 stand . . . part: *fight on either side*   serve: *serve as*
17 breathing: *exercise*

Enter Bertram, Lafeu, and Parolles.

1. Lord. It is the Count Rousillon, my good lord,
Young Bertram.

King.　　　　Youth, thou bear'st thy father's face.
Frank nature, rather curious than in haste,　　　20
Hath well compos'd thee. Thy father's moral parts
Mayst thou inherit too! Welcome to Paris.

Ber. My thanks and duty are your majesty's.

King. I would I had that corporal soundness now, 24
As when thy father and myself in friendship
First tried our soldiership! He did look far
Into the service of the time, and was
Discipled of the bravest: he lasted long;　　　28
But on us both did haggish age steal on,
And wore us out of act. It much repairs me
To talk of your good father. In his youth
He had the wit which I can well observe　　　32
To-day in our young lords; but they may jest
Till their own scorn return to them unnoted
Ere they can hide their levity in honour.
So like a courtier, contempt nor bitterness　　　36
Were in his pride or sharpness; if they were,
His equal had awak'd them; and his honour,
Clock to itself, knew the true minute when
Exception bid him speak, and at this time　　　40
His tongue obey'd his hand: who were below him
He us'd as creatures of another place,
And bow'd his eminent top to their low ranks,

20 Frank: *liberal*　curious: *painstaking*
26, 27 did . . . service: *saw much of the wars*
28 Discipled of: *taught by*
30 wore . . . act: *wore out our ability*　repairs: *refreshes*
33-35 but . . . honour; *cf. n.*　36-38 So . . . them; *cf. n.*
39 Clock to itself: *its own counselor*　true: *proper*
40 Exception: *disapproval*　bid: *bade*
41 obey'd his hand: *obeyed its (the clock's) hand, spoke fittingly*
　who: *those who*

Making them proud of his humility   44
In their poor praise he humbled.   Such a man
Might be a copy to these younger times,
Which, follow'd well, would demonstrate them now
But goers backward.

   Ber.   His good remembrance, sir,   48
Lies richer in your thoughts than on his tomb;
So in approof lives not his epitaph
As in your royal speech.

    King. Would I were with him!   He would always
    say,—   52
Methinks I hear him now: his plausive words
He scatter'd not in ears, but grafted them,
To grow there and to bear,—'Let me not live,'—
This his good melancholy oft began,   56
On the catastrophe and heel of pastime,
When it was out,—'Let me not live,' quoth he,
'After my flame lacks oil, to be the snuff
Of younger spirits, whose apprehensive senses   60
All but new things disdain; whose judgments are
Mere fathers of their garments; whose constancies
Expire before their fashions.'   This he wish'd:
I, after him, do after him wish too,   64
Since I nor wax nor honey can bring home,
I quickly were dissolved from my hive,
To give some labourers room.

   2. Lord.   You're loved, sir;
They that least lend it you shall lack you first.   68

    King. I fill a place, I know 't.   How long is 't, count,
Since the physician at your father's died?

44, 45 Making . . . humbled; *cf. n.*   50, 51 *Cf. n.*
53 plausive: *winning*   55 bear: *bear fruit*
57 On . . . heel: *at the conclusion of*   58 out: *finished*
59 snuff: *object of distaste*   60 apprehensive: *fastidious*
62 Mere . . . garments: *capable merely of devising new fashions*
66 dissolved: *removed*   68 least lend it you: *give you least (love)*

He was much fam'd.
   Ber.   Some six months since, my lord.
   King. If he were living, I would try him yet: **72**
Lend me an arm: the rest have worn me out
With several applications: nature and sickness
Debate it at their leisure.   Welcome, count;
My son's no dearer.
   Ber.   Thank your majesty.   **76**
     Exit [King, attended by all the others]. Flourish.

Scene Three

[Rousillon.   A Room in the Countess's Palace]

Enter Countess, Steward, and Clown.

   Count. I will now hear: what say you of this
gentlewoman?
   Stew. Madam, the care I have had to even
your content, I wish might be found in the **4**
calendar of my past endeavours; for then we
wound our modesty and make foul the clearness
of our deservings, when of ourselves we publish
them.   **8**
   Count. What does this knave here? Get you
gone, sirrah: the complaints I have heard of you
I do not all believe: 'tis my slowness that I do
not; for I know you lack not folly to commit **12**
them, and have ability enough to make such
knaveries yours.
   Clo. 'Tis not unknown to you, madam, I am
a poor fellow.   **16**
   Count. Well, sir.

---

74 several applications: *various remedies*   **75** Debate it: *contend*
3, 4 even your content: *act in accord with your desires*
5 calendar: *catalogue*

Clo. No, madam, 'tis not so well that I am
poor, though many of the rich are damned. But, if
I may have your ladyship's good will to go to the 20
world, Isbel the woman and I will do as we may.

Count. Wilt thou needs be a beggar?

Clo. I do beg your good will in this case.

Count. In what case?   24

Clo. In Isbel's case and mine own. Service is
no heritage; and I think I shall never have the
blessing of God till I have issue o' my body, for
they say barnes are blessings.   28

Count. Tell me thy reason why thou wilt marry.

Clo. My poor body, madam, requires it: I
am driven on by the flesh; and he must needs 32
go that the devil drives.

Count. Is this all your worship's reason?

Clo. Faith, madam, I have other holy reasons,
such as they are.   36

Count. May the world know them?

Clo. I have been, madam, a wicked creature,
as you and all flesh and blood are; and, indeed,
I do marry that I may repent.   40

Count. Thy marriage, sooner than thy
wickedness.

Clo. I am out o' friends, madam; and I hope
to have friends for my wife's sake.   44

Count. Such friends are thine enemies, knave.

Clo. Y'are shallow, madam, in great friends;
for the knaves come to do that for me which I
am aweary of. He that ears my land spares my 48
team, and gives me leave to in the crop: if I be

20, 21 go . . . world: *marry*   21 do . . . may: *do our best*
28 barnes: *children*   35 holy: *religious*
46 shallow . . . friends: *ignorant of the ways of friendship*
48 ears: *plows*   49 in the crop: *gather the harvest*

his cuckold, he's my drudge. He that comforts
my wife is the cherisher of my flesh and blood;
he that cherishes my flesh and blood loves my 52
flesh and blood; he that loves my flesh and
blood is my friend: *ergo,* he that kisses my wife
is my friend. If men could be contented to be
what they are, there were no fear in marriage; 56
for young Charbon the puritan, and old Poysam
the papist, howsome'er their hearts are severed
in religion, their heads are both one; they may
joul horns together like any deer i' the herd.   60

Count. Wilt thou ever be a foul-mouthed and
calumnious knave?

Clo. A prophet I, madam; and I speak the
truth the next way: 64

> 'For I the ballad will repeat,
>   Which men full true shall find:
> Your marriage comes by destiny,
>   Your cuckoo sings by kind.'   68

Count. Get you gone, sir: I'll talk with you
more anon.

Stew. May it please you, madam, that he bid
Helen come to you: of her I am to speak.   72

Count. Sirrah, tell my gentlewoman I would
speak with her; Helen, I mean.

Clo. 'Was this fair face the cause, quoth she,
>   Why the Grecians sacked Troy?   76
> Fond done, done fond,
>   Was this King Priam's joy?
> With that she sighed as she stood,

57, 58 young. . . papist; *cf. n.*   60 joul . . . together; *cf. n.*
64 next: *nearest*   68 cuckoo; *cf. n.*   by kind: *by nature*
77 Fond: *foolishly*

With that she sighed as she stood,   80
   And gave this sentence then;
Among nine bad if one be good,
Among nine bad if one be good,
   There's yet one good in ten.'   84

Count. What! one good in ten? you corrupt
the song, sirrah.

Clo. One good woman in ten, madam; which
is a purifying o' the song. Would God would 88
serve the world so all the year! we'd find no
fault with the tithe-woman if I were the parson.
One in ten, quoth a'! An we might have a good
woman born but o'er every blazing star, or at an 92
earthquake, 'twould mend the lottery well: a
man may draw his heart out ere a' pluck one.

Count. You'll be gone, sir knave, and do as I
command you!   96

Clo. That man should be at woman's command, and yet no hurt done! Though honesty
be no puritan, yet it will do no hurt; it will wear
the surplice of humility over the black gown of a 100
big heart. I am going, forsooth: the business is
for Helen to come hither.   *Exit.*

Count. Well, now.

Stew. I know, madam, you love your gentle- 104
woman entirely.

Count. Faith, I do: her father bequeathed
her to me; and she herself, without other
advantage, may lawfully make title to as much 108
love as she finds: there is more owing her than

92 o'er: *during the appearance of*   blazing star: *comet*
98-101 Though . . . heart; *cf. n.*
101 big: *proud*   business: *thing to be done*
108 make title: *prove her right*

is paid, and more shall be paid her than she'll
demand.

Stew. Madam, I was very late more near her 112
than I think she wished me: alone she was, and
did communicate to herself her own words to her
own ears; she thought, I dare vow for her, they
touched not any stranger sense. Her matter was, 116
she loved your son: Fortune, she said, was no
goddess, that had put such difference betwixt
their two estates; Love no god, that would not
extend his might, only where qualities were level; 120
[Dian no] queen of virgins, that would suffer her
poor knight surprised, without rescue in the first
assault or ransom afterward. This she delivered
in the most bitter touch of sorrow that e'er I 124
heard virgin exclaim in; which I held my duty
speedily to acquaint you withal, sithence in the
loss that may happen it concerns you some-
thing to know it.   128

Count. You have discharged this honestly:
keep it to yourself. Many likelihoods informed
me of this before, which hung so tottering in the
balance that I could neither believe nor mis- 132
doubt. Pray you, leave me: stall this in your bosom; and I thank you for your honest care. I will
speak with you further anon.   *Exit Steward.*

Enter Helen.

Even so it was with me when I was young: 136
  If ever we are nature's, these are ours; this thorn

---

112 late: *recently*
116 touched . . . sense: *were not overheard*   Her matter: *the sub-*
   stance of her speech
122 knight: *votaress*   surprised: *to be surprised*
123 delivered: *spok·*   126 sithence: *since*
127 loss: *misfortune*   132 misdoubt: *disbelieve*
133 stall this: *keep this (knowledge)*   137 these: *these (feelings)*

Doth to our rose of youth rightly belong;
    Our blood to us, this to our blood is born:
It is the show and seal of nature's truth,   140
Where love's strong passion is impress'd in youth:
By our remembrances of days foregone,
Such were our faults, or then we thought them none.
Her eye is sick on 't: I observe her now.   144

    Hel. What is your pleasure, madam?

    Count.   You know, Helen,
I am a mother to you.

    Hel. Mine honourable mistress.

    Count.   Nay, a mother:
Why not a mother? When I said, 'a mother,'   148
Methought you saw a serpent: what's in 'mother'
That you start at it? I say, I am your mother;
And put you in the catalogue of those
That were enwombed mine: 'tis often seen   152
Adoption strives with nature, and choice breeds
A native slip to us from foreign seeds;
You ne'er oppress'd me with a mother's groan,
Yet I express to you a mother's care.   156
God's mercy, maiden! does it curd thy blood
To say I am thy mother? What's the matter,
That this distemper'd messenger of wet,
The many-colour'd Iris, rounds thine eye?   160
Why? that you are my daughter?

    Hel.   That I am not.

    Count. I say, I am your mother.

    Hel.   Pardon, madam;
The Count Rousillon cannot be my brother:
I am from humble, he from honour'd name;   164
No note upon my parents, his all noble:

---

139 blood: *disposition*   140 show: *evidence*
144 on 't: *because of it*   154 native slip: *grafted branch*
159, 160 *Cf. n.*   165 note: *mark of distinction*

My master, my dear lord he is; and I
His servant live, and will his vassal die.
He must not be my brother.
  Count.   Nor I your mother? 168
  Hel. You are my mother, madam: would you were,—
So that my lord your son were not my brother,—
Indeed my mother! or were you both our mothers,
I care no more for than I do for heaven,   172
So I were not his sister. Can't no other,
But, I your daughter, he must be my brother?
  Count. Yes, Helen, you might be my daughter-in-
   law:
God shield you mean it not! daughter and mother 176
So strive upon your pulse. What, pale again?
My fear hath catch'd your fondness: now I see
The mystery of your loveliness, and find
Your salt tears' head: now to all sense 'tis gross: 180
You love my son: invention is asham'd,
Against the proclamation of thy passion,
To say thou dost not: therefore tell me true;
But tell me then, 'tis so: for, look, thy cheeks 184
Confess it, th' one to th' other; and thine eyes
See it so grossly shown in thy behaviours
That in their kind they speak it: only sin
And hellish obstinacy tie thy tongue,   188
That truth should be suspected. Speak, is 't so?
If it be so, you have wound a goodly clew;
If it be not, forswear 't: howe'er, I charge thee,
As heaven shall work in me for thine avail, 192

173 Can't no other: *can it not be otherwise*
177 strive . . . pulse: *affect your pulse in turn*
178 catch'd: *discovered*   180 head: *source* gross: *palpable*
181 invention: *dissimulation*   182 Against: *in the face of*
186 grossly: *openly*   187 in their kind: *after their own manner*
189 That . . . suspected: *in order to cast doubt upon the truth*
190 wound . . . clew: *made a fine snarl* 191 howe'er: *in any event*
192 *If you wish Heaven to move me to help you*

To tell me truly.

    Hel.   Good madam, pardon me!

    Count. Do you love my son?

    Hel.   Your pardon, noble mistress!

    Count. Love you my son?

    Hel.   Do not you love him, madam?

    Count. Go not about; my love hath in 't a bond   **196**
Whereof the world takes note: come, come, disclose
The state of your affection, for your passions
Have to the full appeach'd.

    Hel.   Then, I confess,
Here on my knee, before high heaven and you   **200**
That before you, and next unto high heaven,
I love your son.
My friends were poor, but honest; so's my love:
Be not offended, for it hurts not him   **204**
That he is lov'd of me: I follow him not
By any token of presumptuous suit;
Nor would I have him till I do deserve him;
Yet never know how that desert should be.   **208**
I know I love in vain, strive against hope;
Yet, in this captious and intenible sieve
I still pour in the waters of my love,
And lack not to lose still. Thus, Indian-like,   **212**
Religious in mine error, I adore
The sun, that looks upon his worshipper,
But knows of him no more. My dearest madam,
Let not your hate encounter with my love   **216**
For loving where you do: but, if yourself,
Whose aged honour cites a virtuous youth,
Did ever in so true a flame of liking
Wish chastely and love dearly, that your Dian   **220**

196 Go not about: *do not quibble*   199 appeach'd: *accused you*
210 captious: *deceptive*   intenible: *incapable of retaining*
212 lack . . . still: *have an inexhaustible supply to pour forth*
216 encounter with: *oppose*   218 cites: *is proof of*

Was both herself and Love, O! then, give pity
To her, whose state is such that cannot choose
But lend and give where she is sure to lose,
That seeks not to find that her search implies,   224
But, riddle-like, lives sweetly where she dies.

    Count. Had you not lately an intent—speak truly—
To go to Paris?

    Hel.   Madam, I had.

    Count.   Wherefore? tell true.

    Hel. I will tell truth; by grace itself I swear.   228
You know my father left me some prescriptions
Of rare and prov'd effects, such as his reading
And manifest experience had collected
For general sovereignty; and that he will'd me   232
In heedfull'st reservation to bestow them,
As notes whose faculties inclusive were
More than they were in note.   Amongst the rest,
There is a remedy, approv'd, set down   236
To cure the desperate languishings whereof
The king is render'd lost.

    Count.   This was your motive
For Paris, was it? speak.

    Hel. My lord your son made me to think of this; 240
Else Paris and the medicine and the king
Had from the conversation of my thoughts
Haply been absent then.

    Count.   But think you, Helen,
If you should tender your supposed aid,   244
He would receive it?   He and his physicians
Are of a mind; he, that they cannot help him,

---

224 that: *that which*   225 riddle-like: *paradoxically*
232 general sovereignty: *universal efficacy*
233 reservation: *safe-keeping*
234 notes: *prescriptions*   faculties: *powers*   inclusive: *all-embracing*
235 in note: *stated in writing*
238 render'd lost: *reported to be sick unto death*
242 conversation: *intercourse*   243 Haply: *perhaps*

They, that they cannot help.   How shall they credit
A poor unlearned virgin, when the schools,   248
Embowell'd of their doctrine, have left off
The danger to itself?

    Hel.   There's something in 't,
More than my father's skill, which was the great'st
Of his profession, that his good receipt   252
Shall for my legacy be sanctified
By the luckiest stars in heaven: and, would your honour
But give me leave to try success, I'd venture
The well-lost life of mine on his Grace's cure,   256
By such a day, an hour.

    Count.   Dost thou believe 't?

    Hel. Ay, madam, knowingly.

    Count. Why, Helen, thou shalt have my leave **and**
      love,
Means, and attendants, and my loving greetings   260
To those of mine in court.   I'll stay at home
And pray God's blessing into thy attempt.
Be gone to-morrow; and be sure of this,
What I can help thee to thou shalt not miss.   264

                                 Exeunt.

249 Embowell'd . . . doctrine: *exhausted of their learning*
    left off: *abandoned*   261 those of mine: *my kinsmen*
262 into: *upon*

ACT SECOND

Scene One

[Paris. A Room in the King's Palace]

*Enter the King, [attended,] with divers young Lords
    taking leave for the Florentine war; Count Rou-
    sillon and Parolles. Flourish [of] cornets.*

King. Farewell, young lords: these warlike prin-
        ciples
Do not throw from you: and you, my lords, farewell:
Share the advice betwixt you; if both gain all,
The gift doth stretch itself as 'tis receiv'd,   4
And is enough for both.
    1. Lord.   'Tis our hope, sir,
After well enter'd soldiers, to return
And find your Grace in health.
    King. No, no, it cannot be; and yet my heart   8
Will not confess he owes the malady
That doth my life besiege.   Farewell, young lords;
Whether I live or die, be you the sons
Of worthy Frenchmen: let higher Italy—   12
Those bated that inherit but the fall
Of the last monarchy—see that you come
Not to woo honour, but to wed it; when
The bravest questant shrinks, find what you seek   16
That fame may cry you loud: I say, farewell.
    2. Lord. Health, at your bidding, serve your maj-
        esty!
    King. Those girls of Italy, take heed of them:
They say our French lack language to deny   20

6 After . . . soldiers: *after we are well embarked on our military
    careers*   9 owes: *owns*
12-14 let . . . monarchy; *cf. n.*   16 questant: *seeker*
17 cry you loud: *proclaim you loudly*

If they demand: beware of being captives,
Before you serve.

    Both Lords.   Our hearts receive your warnings.

    King. Farewell. [*To another Lord.*] Come hither to
      me.   [*They converse.*]

    1. Lord. [*To Bertram.*] O my sweet lord, that you
      will stay behind us!   24

    Par. 'Tis not his fault, the spark.

    2. Lord.   O, 'tis brave wars!

    Par. Most admirable: I have seen those wars.

    Ber. I am commanded here, and kept a coil with
'Too young,' and 'the next year,' and ''tis too early.' 28

    Par. An thy mind stand to 't, boy, steal away
      bravely.

    Ber. I shall stay here the forehorse to a smock,
Creaking my shoes on the plain masonry,
Till honour be bought up and no sword worn   32
But one to dance with! By heaven! I'll steal away.

    1. Lord. There's honour in the theft.

    Par.   Commit it, count.

    2. Lord. I am your accessary; and so farewell.

    Ber. I grow to you, and our parting is a tor- 36
tured body.

    1. Lord. Farewell, captain.

    2. Lord. Sweet Monsieur Parolles!

    Par. Noble heroes, my sword and yours are 40
kin. Good sparks and lustrous, a word, good
metals: you shall find in the regiment of the
Spinii, one Captain Spurio, with his cicatrice,
an emblem of war, here on his sinister cheek: it 44
was this very sword entrenched it: say to him,
I live, and observe his reports for me.

27 kept a coil: *pestered*   30 forehorse . . . smock: *usher to a lady*
32 bought up: *entirely appropriated by others*
33 But . . . with; *cf. n.*   35 accessary: *accessory*
36, 37 our . . . body; *cf. n.*

2. Lord. We shall, noble captain.

Par. Mars dote on you for his novices! 48

[*Exeunt Lords.*]

What will ye do?

Ber. Stay the king.

Par. Use a more spacious ceremony to the
noble lords; you have restrained yourself within 52
the list of too cold an adieu: be more expressive
to them; for they wear themselves in the cap of
the time, there do muster true gait, eat, speak,
and move under the influence of the most re- 56
ceived star; and though the devil lead the measure, such are to be followed. After them, and
take a more dilated farewell.

Ber. And I will do so.   60

Par. Worthy fellows; and like to prove
most sinewy swordmen.

Exeunt [*Bertram and Parolles*].

Enter Lafeu.

Laf. [*Kneeling.*] Pardon, my lord, for me and for
my tidings.

King. I'll see thee to stand up.   64

Laf. Then here's a man stands that has brought his
pardon.

I would you had kneel'd, my lord, to ask me mercy,
And that at my bidding you could so stand up.

King. I would I had, so I had broke thy pate, 68
And ask'd thee mercy for 't.

Laf. Good faith, across: but, my good lord, 'tis thus;
Will you be cur'd of your infirmity?

48 novices: *devotees*   49 ye: *i.e. Bertram*
50 Stay the king: *await the king's pleasure*
51 spacious ceremony: *elaborate courtesy*   53 list: *boundary*
54, 55 wear . . . time: *are an ornament to the time*
55 muster . . . gait: *exhibit good manners*
56 received: *fashionable*   64 I'll . . . to: *I wish to see you*

King. No.   72
  Laf. O! will you eat no grapes, my royal fox?
Yes, but you will my noble grapes an if
My royal fox could reach them.   I have seen a medicine
That's able to breathe life into a stone,   76
Quicken a rock, and make you dance canary
With spritely fire and motion; whose simple touch
Is powerful to araise King Pepin, nay,
To give great Charlemain a pen in's hand   80
And write to her a love-line.
    King.   What 'her' is this?
  Laf. Why, Doctor She.   My lord, there's one arriv'd,
If you will see her: now, by my faith and honour,
If seriously I may convey my thoughts   84
In this my light deliverance, I have spoke
With one, that in her sex, her years, profession,
Wisdom, and constancy, hath amaz'd me more
Than I dare blame my weakness.   Will you see her   88
(For that is her demand) and know her business?
That done, laugh well at me.
    King.   Now, good Lafeu,
Bring in the admiration, that we with thee
May spend our wonder too, or take off thine   92
By wondering how thou took'st it.
    Laf.   Nay, I'll fit you,
And not be all day neither.

                        [*He retires to the door.*]
  King. Thus he his special nothing ever prologues.
  Laf. [*to Helena, without.*] Nay, come your ways.

                        Enter Helen.

    King.   This haste hath wings indeed. 96

---

77 canary: *a lively dunce*   85 deliverance: *speech*
87, 88 more . . . weakness; *cf. n.*   91 admiration: *marvel*
92 take off: *dispel*   93 took'st: *didst conceive*   fit: *satisfy*
95 *Thus he always introduces the particular nonsense he has in hand*

Laf. Nay, come your ways;
This is his majesty, say your mind to him:
A traitor you do look like, but such traitors
His majesty seldom fears: I am Cressid's uncle,   100
That dare leave two together.   Fare you well.

                                              Exit.

King. Now, fair one, does your business follow us?
Hel. Ay, my good lord.
Gerard de Narbon was my father;   104
In what he did profess well found.
    King.   I knew him.
    Hel. The rather will I spare my praises towards him;
Knowing him is enough.   On's bed of death
Many receipts he gave me; chiefly one,   108
Which, as the dearest issue of his practice,
And of his old experience the only darling,
He bade me store up as a triple eye,
Safer than mine own two, more dear.   I have so; 112
And, hearing your high majesty is touch'd
With that malignant cause wherein the honour
Of my dear father's gift stands chief in power,
I come to tender it and my appliance,   116
With all bound humbleness.
    King.   We thank you, maiden,
But may not be so credulous of cure,
When our most learned doctors leave us, and
The congregated college have concluded   120
That labouring art can never ransom nature
From her inaidable estate; I say we must not
So stain our judgment or corrupt our hope,

102 follow: *concern*   105 well found: *learned*
111 triple: *third*   114 cause: *disease*
114, 115 wherein . . . power; *cf. n.*
116 appliance: *application (of the medicine)*
117 bound: *dutiful*
120 congregated college: *entire college (of physicians) in consultation*
122 inaidable: *incurable*

To prostitute our past-cure malady   **124**
To empirics, or to dissever so
Our great self and our credit, to esteem
A senseless help when help past sense we deem.

    Hel. My duty then, shall pay me for my pains: **128**
I will no more enforce mine office on you;
Humbly entreating from your royal thoughts
A modest one to bear me back again.

    King. I cannot give thee less, to be call'd grateful. **132**
Thou thought'st to help me, and such thanks I give
As one near death to those that wish him live;
But what at full I know, thou know'st no part,
I knowing all my peril, thou no art.   **136**

    Hel. What I can do can do no hurt to try,
Since you set up your rest 'gainst remedy.
He that of greatest works is finisher
Oft does them by the weakest minister: **140**
So holy writ in babes hath judgment shown,
When judges have been babes; great floods have flown
From simple sources, and great seas have dried
When miracles have by the greatest been denied.   **144**
Oft expectation fails, and most oft there
Where most it promises; and oft it hits
Where hope is coldest and despair most sits.

    King. I must not hear thee: fare thee well, kind
        maid.   **148**
Thy pains, not us'd, must by thyself be paid:
Proffers not took reap thanks for their reward.

    Hel. Inspired merit so by breath is barr'd.
It is not so with Him that all things knows,   **152**
As 'tis with us that square our guess by shows;

125 empirics: *charlatans*
127 past sense: *beyond reasonable expectation*
132 to be call'd: *if I am to be called*
138 *Since you are so sure there is no remedy*   151 breath: *words*
153 square . . . shows: *test our impressions by outward appearances*

But most it is presumption in us when
The help of heaven we count the act of men.
Dear sir, to my endeavours give consent;   **156**
Of heaven, not me, make an experiment.
I am not an imposture that proclaim
Myself against the level of mine aim;
But know I think, and think I know most sure   **160**
My art is not past power nor you past cure.

    King. Art thou so confident?   Within what space
Hop'st thou my cure?
    Hel.   The greatest grace lending **grace,**
Ere twice the horses of the sun shall bring   **164**
Their fiery torcher his diurnal ring,
Ere twice in murk and occidental damp
Moist Hesperus hath quench'd her sleepy lamp,
Or four and twenty times the pilot's glass   **168**
Hath told the thievish minutes how they pass,
What is infirm from your sound parts shall fly,
Health shall live free and sickness freely die.

    King. Upon thy certainty and confidence   **172**
What dar'st thou venture?
    Hel.   Tax of impudence,
A strumpet's boldness, a divulged shame,
Traduc'd by odious ballads: my maiden's name
Sear'd otherwise; nay worse—if worse—extended **176**
With vilest torture let my life be ended.

    King. Methinks in thee some blessed spirit doth
      speak
His powerful sound within an organ weak;
And what impossibility would slay   **180**
In common sense, sense saves another way.
Thy life is dear; for all that life can rate

159 against . . . aim: *equal to my task*
165 diurnal ring: *daily round*   167 her; *cf. n.*
168 glass: *hour-glass*   169 told: *counted*   173 Tax: *accusation*
176 nay . . . worse; *cf. n.*   182 rate: *consider*

Worth name of life, in thee hath estimate;
Youth, beauty, wisdom, courage, all   184
That happiness and prime can happy call:
Thou this to hazard needs must intimate
Skill infinite or monstrous desperate.
Sweet practiser, thy physic I will try,   188
That ministers thine own death if I die.

   Hel. If I break time, or flinch in property
Of what I spoke, unpitied let me die,
And well deserv'd.   Not helping, death's my fee;   192
But, if I help, what do you promise me?
   King. Make thy demand.
   Hel.   But will you make it even?
   King. Ay, by my sceptre, and my hopes of heaven.
   Hel. Then shalt thou give me with thy kingly
     hand   196
What husband in thy power I will command:
Exempted be from me the arrogance
To choose from forth the royal blood of France,
My low and humble name to propagate   200
With any branch or image of thy state;
But such a one, thy vassal, whom I know
Is free for me to ask, thee to bestow.

   King. Here is my hand; the premises observ'd,   204
Thy will by my performance shall be serv'd:
So make the choice of thy own time, for I,
Thy resolv'd patient, on thee still rely.
More should I question thee, and more I must,   208
(Though more to know could not be more to trust)
From whence thou cam'st, how tended on; but rest

183 in . . . estimate: *has great value for you*   185 prime: *youth*
186 Thou . . . hazard: *your risking this*   intimate: *indicate*
188 practiser: *practitioner*
190 *If I delay beyond the appointed time, or come short in performance*
194 make it even: *fulfill it*
198 Exempted be: *far be*   210 tended on: *attended*

Unquestion'd welcome and undoubted blest.
Give me some help here, ho! If thou proceed   212
As high as word, my deed shall match thy deed.

Flourish. Exit [with Attendants;
Helena follows.]

Scene Two

[*Rousillon. A Room in the Countess's Palace*]

Enter Countess and Clown.

Count. Come on, sir; I shall now put you to
the height of your breeding.

Clo. I will show myself highly fed and lowly
taught. I know my business is but to the   4
court.

Count. To the court! why what place make
you special, when you put off that with such
contempt? 'But to the court!'   8

Clo. Truly, madam, if God have lent a man
any manners, he may easily put it off at court.
He that cannot make a leg, put off's cap, kiss his
hand, and say nothing, has neither leg, hands, 12
lip, nor cap; and indeed such a fellow, to say
precisely, were not for the court: but for me, I
have an answer will serve all men.

Count. Marry, that's a bountiful answer 16
that fits all questions.

Clo. It is like a barber's chair that fits all
buttocks; the pin-buttock, the quatch-buttock,
the brawn-buttock, or any buttock.   20

212, 213 If . . . word: *if you perform your promises*
1, 2 put . . . height: *make thorough trial*
6, 7 make you special: *do you consider extraordinary*
10 put it off: *make his way*   11 leg: *bow*
19 pin-buttock: *thin buttock*   quatch-buttock: *flat buttock*
20 brawn-buttock: *brawny buttock*

Count. Will your answer serve fit to all questions?

Clo. As fit as ten groats is for the hand of an attorney, as your French crown for your taffeta 24 punk, as Tib's rush for Tom's forefinger, as a pancake for Shrove-Tuesday, a morris for May-day, as the nail to his hole, the cuckold to his horn, as a scolding quean to a wrangling knave, 28 as the nun's lip to the friar's mouth, nay, as the pudding to his skin.

Count. Have you, I say, an answer of such fitness for all questions?   32

Clo. From below your duke to beneath your constable, it will fit any question.

Count. It must be an answer of most mon-strous size that must fit all demands.   36

Clo. But a trifle neither, in good faith, if the learned should speak truth of it.   Here it is, and all that belongs to 't; ask me if I am a courtier; it shall do you no harm to learn.   40

Count. To be young again, if we could!   I will be a fool in question, hoping to be the wiser by your answer.   I pray you, sir, are you a cour-tier?   44

Clo. O Lord, sir! there's a simple putting off. More, more, a hundred of them.

Count. Sir, I am a poor friend of yours, that loves you.   48

Clo. O Lord, sir!   Thick, thick, spare not me.

Count. I think, sir, you can eat none of this homely meat.   52

24 crown: *a coin*   24, 25 taffeta punk: *prostitute dressed in taffeta*
25 Tib's . . . forefinger; *cf. n.*   26 morris: *morris-dance*
28 quean: *woman*   52 homely meat: *humble food*

Clo. O Lord, sir! Nay, put me to 't, I warrant you.

Count. You were lately whipped, sir, as I think.   56

Clo. O Lord, sir! Spare not me.

Count. Do you cry, 'O Lord, sir!' at your whipping, and 'Spare not me'? Indeed your 'O Lord, sir!' is very sequent to your whipping: 60 you would answer very well to a whipping, if you were but bound to 't.

Clo. I ne'er had worse luck in my life in my 'O Lord, sir!' I see things may serve long, but 64 not serve ever.

Count. I play the noble housewife with the time,
To entertain 't so merrily with a fool.

Clo. O Lord, sir! why, there 't serves well again.   68

Count. An end, sir: to your business. Give Helen this,
And urge her to a present answer back:
Commend me to my kinsmen and my son.
This is not much.   72

Clo. Not much commendation to them?

Count. Not much employment for you: you understand me.

Clo. Most fruitfully: I am there before my legs.

Count. Haste you again.   76

Exeunt [*severally*].

60 very sequent to: *a natural outcome of*
62 bound to 't: *obliged to*   66 *I am indeed provident of my time*
67 entertain 't: *occupy it*   75 fruitfully: *fully*

Scene Three

[Paris.   A Room in the King's Palace]

Enter Count, Lafeu, and Parolles.

Laf. They say miracles are past; and we have
our philosophical persons, to make modern and
familiar, things supernatural and causeless.
Hence is it that we make trifles of terrors, en- 4
sconcing ourselves into seeming knowledge, when
we should submit ourselves to an unknown fear.

Par. Why, 'tis the rarest argument of wonder
that hath shot out in our latter times. 8

Ber. And so 'tis.

Laf. To be relinquished of the artists,—

Par. So I say—both of Galen and Paracelsus.

Laf. Of all the learned and authentic fellows,— 12

Par. Right; so I say.

Laf. That gave him out incurable,—

Par. Why, there 'tis; so say I too.

Laf. Not to be helped,— 16

Par. Right; as 'twere, a man assured of a—

Laf. Uncertain life, and sure death.

Par. Just, you say well: so would I have
said. 20

Laf. I may truly say it is a novelty to the
world.

Par. It is, indeed: if you will have it in
showing, you shall read it in What-do-you-call 24
there.

2 modern: *trivial*
4, 5 ensconcing . . . into: *sheltering ourselves within*
10 relinquished . . . artists: *given up by all the scholars*
12 authentic: *authoritative*   fellows: *members (of the college of
           physicians)*
                                      14 gave him out: *pronounced him*
19 Just: *precisely*   23, 24 in showing: *in black and white*

Laf. A showing of a heavenly effect in an earthly actor.

Par. That's it I would have said; the very same. **28**

Laf. Why, your dolphin is not lustier: 'fore me, I speak in respect—

Par. Nay, 'tis strange, 'tis very strange, that is the brief and the tedious of it; and he's of a most facinerious spirit that will not acknowledge it to be the— **32**

Laf. Very hand of heaven— **36**

Par. Ay, so I say.

Laf. In a most weak—

Par. And debile minister, great power, great transcendence: which should, indeed, give us a further use to be made than alone the recovery of the king, as to be— **40**

Laf. Generally thankful. **44**

> *Enter King, Helen, and Attendants.*

Par. I would have said it; you say well. Here comes the king.

Laf. Lustig, as the Dutchman says: I'll like a maid the better, whilst I have a tooth in my head. Why, he's able to lead her a coranto. **48**

Par. Mort du vinaigre! Is not this Helen?

Laf. 'Fore God, I think so.

King. Go, call before me all the lords in court. **52**

> *[Exit an Attendant.]*

Sit, my preserver, by thy patient's side:
And with this healthful hand, whose banish'd sense
Thou hast repeal'd, a second time receive

34 facinerious; *cf. n.*
49 coranto: *a lively dance*
54 sense: *faculties*

47 Lustig: *brisk*
50 Mort du vinaigre; *cf. n.*
55 repeal'd: *called back*

The confirmation of my promised gift,   56
Which but attends thy naming.

                    Enter three or four Lords.

Fair maid, send forth thine eye: this youthful parcel
Of noble bachelors stand at my bestowing,
O'er whom both sovereign power and father's voice   60
I have to use; thy frank election make;
Thou hast power to choose, and they none to forsake.

    Hel. To each of you one fair and virtuous mistress
Fall, when Love please; marry, to each but one.   64

    Laf. I'd give bay Curtal, and his furniture,
My mouth no more were broken than these boys'
And writ as little beard.

    King.   Peruse them well:
Not one of those but had a noble father.   68

                              She addresses her to a Lord.

    Hel. Gentlemen,
Heaven hath through me restor'd the king to health.

    All. We understand it, and thank heaven for you.

    Hel. I am a simple maid, and therein wealthiest   72
That I protest I simply am a maid.
Please it your majesty, I have done already:
The blushes in my cheeks thus whisper me,
'We blush, that thou shouldst choose; but, be refus'd, 76
Let the white death sit on thy cheek for ever;
We'll ne'er come there again.'

    King.   Make choice, and see;
Who shuns thy love, shuns all his love in me.

    Hel. Now, Dian, from thy altar do I fly,   80
And to imperial Love, that god most high,

57 attends: *awaits*   58 parcel: *group*
62 forsake: *deny*   64 to . . . one; *cf. n.*
65 bay . . . furniture: *my bay horse and his harness*
66 broken: *lacking teeth*   67 writ: *laid claim to*
77 white death: *deathly pallor*

Do my sighs stream.   Sir, will you hear my suit?

1. Lord. And grant it.

Hel.   Thanks, sir; all the rest is mute.

   Laf. I had rather be in this choice than   84
throw ames-ace for my life.

Hel. The honour, sir, that flames in your fair eyes,
Before I speak, too threateningly replies:
Love make your fortunes twenty times above   88
Her that so wishes, and her humble love!

   2. Lord. No better, if you please.

Hel.   My wish receive,
Which great Love grant! and so I take my leave.

   Laf. Do all they deny her?   An they were   92
sons of mine, I'd have them whipp'd or I would
send them to the Turk to make eunuchs of.

Hel. [*To third Lord.*] Be not afraid that I your
   hand should take;
I'll never do you wrong, for your own sake: 96
Blessing upon your vows; and in your bed
Find fairer fortune, if you ever wed!

   Laf. These boys are boys of ice, they'll none
have her: sure, they are bastards to the Eng-   100
lish; the French ne'er got 'em.

Hel. You are too young, too happy, and too good,
To make yourself a son out of my blood.

   4. Lord. Fair one, I think not so.   104

   Laf. There's one grape yet.   I am sure thy
father drunk wine.   But if thou be'st not an ass,
I am a youth of fourteen: I have known thee
already.   108

Hel. [*To Bertram.*] I dare not say I take you; but
   I give

83 all . . . mute: *you assent with your lips only*   84, 85 *Cf. n.*

Me and my service, ever whilst I live,
Into your guiding power.   This is the man.

   King. Why then, young Bertram, take her; she's thy
    wife.   112

   Ber. My wife, my liege!   I shall beseech your high-
    ness
In such a business give me leave to use
The help of mine own eyes.

   King.   Know'st thou not, Bertram,
What she has done for me?

   Ber.   Yes, my good lord;   116
But never hope to know why I should marry her.

   King. Thou know'st she has rais'd me from my
    sickly bed.

   Ber. But follows it, my lord, to bring me down
Must answer for your raising? I know her well: 120
She had her breeding at my father's charge.
A poor physician's daughter my wife!   Disdain
Rather corrupt me ever!

   King. 'Tis only title thou disdain'st in her, the
    which   124
I can build up.   Strange is it that our bloods,
Of colour, weight, and heat, pour'd all together,
Would quite confound distinction, yet stands off
In differences so mighty.   If she be   128
All that is virtuous, save what thou dislik'st,
A poor physician's daughter, thou dislik'st
Of virtue for the name; but do not so:
From lowest place when virtuous things proceed,   132
The place is dignified by the doer's deed:

122, 123 Disdain . . . ever: *rather let your displeasure cast me down
forever*   124 title: *want of title*
126 Of: *in respect of*
127 confound distinction: *defy differentiation*   stands off: *diverge*
130, 131 thou . . . name: *you despise virtue because it lacks a high-
sounding title*

Where great additions swell's, and virtue none,
It is a dropsied honour.   Good alone
Is good, without a name: vileness is so: 136
The property by what it is should go,
Not by the title.   She is young, wise, fair;
In these to nature she's immediate heir,
And these breed honour: that is honour's scorn   140
Which challenges itself as honour's born,
And is not like the sire: honours thrive
When rather from our acts we them derive
Than our foregoers.   The mere word's a slave,   144
Debosh'd on every tomb, on every grave,
A lying trophy, and as oft is dumb
Where dust and damn'd oblivion is the tomb
Of honour'd bones indeed.   What should be said?   148
If thou canst like this creature as a maid,
I can create the rest: virtue and she
Is her own dower; honour and wealth from me.

    Ber. I cannot love her, nor will strive to do 't.   152

    King. Thou wrong'st thyself if thou shouldst strive
      to choose.

    Hel. That you are well restor'd, my lord, I'm glad:
Let the rest go.

    King. My honour's at the stake, which to defeat 156
I must produce my power.   Here, take her hand,
Proud scornful boy, unworthy this good gift,
That dost in vile misprision shackle up
My love and her desert; that canst not dream   160

134 *When great titles exalt us, yet we have no virtue*
135 dropsied: *swollen by disease*
136 vileness is so: *vileness is vileness, although it be not called so*
137 property: *quality*
139 *She is indebted to nature for these gifts*
141 challenges: *proclaims*   144 foregoers: *ancestors*
145 Debosh'd: *perverted*
156 which to defeat: *to prevent the loss of which*
159 misprision; *cf. n.*

We, poising us in her defective scale,
Shall weigh thee to the beam; that wilt not know,
It is in us to plant thine honour where
We please to have it grow. Check thy contempt: 164
Obey our will, which travails in thy good:
Believe not thy disdain, but presently
Do thine own fortunes that obedient right
Which both thy duty owes and our power claims; 168
Or I will throw thee from my care for ever
Into the staggers and the careless lapse
Of youth and ignorance, both my revenge and hate
Loosing upon thee, in the name of justice, 172
Without all terms of pity. Speak; thine answer.

   Ber. Pardon, my gracious lord; for I submit
My fancy to your eyes. When I consider
What great creation and what dole of honour 176
Flies where you bid it, I find that she, which late
Was in my nobler thoughts most base, is now
The praised of the king; who, so ennobled,
Is, as 'twere, born so.

   King.   Take her by the hand, 180
And tell her she is thine: to whom I promise
A counterpoise, if not to thy estate
A balance more replete.

   Ber.   I take her hand.

   King. Good fortune and the favour of the king 184
Smile upon this contract, whose ceremony
Shall seem expedient on the now-born brief,
And be perform'd to-night: the solemn feast
Shall more attend upon the coming space, 188

161 poising us: *adding our weight*   defective: *light*
163 in us: *in our power*   165 travails in: *works toward*
167 *Serve your own interests by obedience*
170 staggers: *bewilderment*   careless lapse: *unheeded fall*
178 nobler: *too noble*   183 more replete: *more than equal*
186 *Shall seem to follow immediately upon this new-made contract*

Expecting absent friends. As thou lov'st her,
Thy love's to me religious; else, does err.

> *Exeunt [King, Bertram, Helena, Lords, and*
> *Attendants.] Parolles and Lafeu stay be-*
> *hind, commenting of this wedding.*

Laf. Do you hear, monsieur? a word with you.

Par. Your pleasure, sir?   192

Laf. Your lord and master did well to make
his recantation.

Par. Recantation! My lord! my master!

Laf. Ay; is it not a language I speak?   196

Par. A most harsh one, and not to be understood without bloody succeeding. My master!

Laf. Are you companion to the Count
Rousillon?   200

Par. To any count; to all counts; to what is
man.

Laf. To what is count's man: count's master
is of another style.   204

Par. You are too old, sir; let it satisfy you,
you are too old.

Laf. I must tell thee, sirrah, I write man; to
which title age cannot bring thee.   208

Par. What I dare too well do, I dare not do.

Laf. I did think thee, for two ordinaries,
to be a pretty wise fellow: thou didst make
tolerable vent of thy travel; it might pass; yet 212
the scarfs and the bannerets about thee did
manifoldly dissuade me from believing thee a
vessel of too great a burthen. I have now found
thee; when I lose thee again, I care not; yet art 216

189 Expecting: *tarrying for*   198 succeeding: *consequences*
207 write: *call myself*   210 ordinaries: *meals*
212 vent: *display*   215, 216 found thee: *found you out*

thou good for nothing but taking up, and that
thou'rt scarce worth.

Par. Hadst thou not the privilege of an-
tiquity upon thee,—   220

Laf. Do not plunge thyself too far in anger,
lest thou hasten thy trial; which if—Lord have
mercy on thee for a hen! So, my good window
of lattice, fare thee well: thy casement I need 224
not open, for I look through thee. Give me thy
hand.

Par. My lord, you give me most egregious
indignity.   228

Laf. Ay, with all my heart; and thou art
worthy of it.

Par. I have not, my lord, deserved it.

Laf. Yes, good faith, every dram of it; and I 232
will not bate thee a scruple.

Par. Well, I shall be wiser—

Laf. Ev'n as soon as thou canst, for thou
hast to pull at a smack o' the contrary. If ever 236
thou be'st bound in thy scarf and beaten, thou
shalt find what it is to be proud of thy bondage.
I have a desire to hold my acquaintance with
thee, or rather my knowledge, that I may say in 240
the default, he is a man I know.

Par. My lord, you do me most insupportable
vexation.

Laf. I would it were hell-pains for thy sake, 244
and my poor doing eternal: for doing I am past;
as I will by thee, in what motion age will give
me leave.   *Exit.*

217 taking up: *contradicting (used punningly)*
223 hen: *coward*   234 *Cf. n.*
236 pull . . . contrary: *draw at a taste of the opposite quality (folly)*
240, 241 in the default: *when it is necessary*   246 as . . . thee; *cf. n.*
246, 247 in . . . leave: *as fast as my age permits*

Par. Well, thou hast a son shall take this 248
disgrace off me; scurvy, old, filthy, scurvy lord!
Well, I must be patient; there is no fettering of
authority.   I'll beat him, by my life, if I can
meet him with any convenience, an he were 252
double and double a lord.   I'll have no more pity
of his age than I would have of—I'll beat him,
an if I could but meet him again!

[*Re-*]*enter Lafeu.*

Laf. Sirrah, your lord and master's married; 256
there's news for you: you have a new mistress.

Par. I most unfeignedly beseech your lordship to make some reservation of your wrongs:
he is my good lord: whom I serve above is my 260
master.

Laf. Who? God?

Par. Ay, sir.

Laf. The devil it is that's thy master.   Why 264
dost thou garter up thy arms o' this fashion?
dost make hose of thy sleeves? do other servants
so?   Thou wert best set thy lower part where thy
nose stands.   By mine honour, if I were but two 268
hours younger, I'd beat thee: methinks thou art
a general offence, and every man should beat
thee: I think thou wast created for men to
breathe themselves upon thee.   272

Par. This is hard and undeserved measure,
my lord.

Laf. Go to, sir; you were beaten in Italy for
picking a kernel out of a pomegranate; you are 276
a vagabond and no true traveller: you are more
saucy with lords and honourable personages

272 breathe: *exercise*

than the commission of your birth and virtue gives
you heraldry. You are not worth another 280
word, else I'd call you knave. I leave you.   *Exit.*

Enter Count Rousillon.

Par. Good, very good; it is so then: good,
very good, let it be concealed awhile.

Ber. Undone, and forfeited to cares for ever!   284

Par. What's the matter, sweet heart?

Ber. Although before the solemn priest I have sworn,
I will not bed her.

Par. What, what, sweet heart?   288

Ber. O my Parolles, they have married me!
I'll to the Tuscan wars, and never bed her.

Par. France is a dog-hole, and it no more merits
The tread of a man's foot. To the wars!   292

Ber. There's letters from my mother: what the import is
I know not yet.

Par. Ay, that would be known. To the wars, my
boy! to the wars!

He wears his honour in a box, unseen,   296
That hugs his kicky-wicky here at home,
Spending his manly marrow in her arms,
Which should sustain the bound and high curvet
Of Mars's fiery steed. To other regions   300
France is a stable; we that dwell in 't jades;
Therefore, to the war!

Ber. It shall be so: I'll send her to my house,
Acquaint my mother with my hate to her,   304
And wherefore I am fled; write to the king
That which I durst not speak: his present gift

279 commission: *warrant*   280 heraldry: *rank*
284 forfeited: *given up*   299 curvet: *leap*
301 jades: *draft-horses*

Shall furnish me to those Italian fields,
Where noble fellows strike. Wars is no strife   308
To the dark house and the detested wife.

Par. Will this capriccio hold in thee? art sure?

Ber. Go with me to my chamber and advise me.
I'll send her straight away: to-morrow   312
I'll to the wars, she to her single sorrow.

Par. Why, these balls bound; there's noise in it.
'Tis hard:
A young man married is a man that's marr'd:
Therefore away, and leave her bravely; go: 316
The king has done you wrong: but, hush! 'tis so.

Exit [with Bertram].

Scene Four

[Same.   Another Room in the Palace]

Enter Helena and Clown.

Hel. My mother greets me kindly: is she well?

Clo. She is not well; but yet she has her
health; she's very merry, but yet she is not
well: but thanks be given, she's very well, and 4
wants nothing i' the world; but yet she is not
well.

Hel. If she be very well, what does she ail
that she's not very well?   8

Clo. Truly, she's very well indeed, but for
two things.

Hel. What two things?

Clo. One, that she's not in heaven, whither 12

307 furnish me to: *equip me for*   309 To: *compared to*
310 capriccio: *whim*   hold: *persist*   314 these . . . it; *cf. n.*
7 what: *in what way*

God send her quickly! the other, that she's in
earth, from whence God send her quickly!

Enter Parolles.

Par. Bless you, my fortunate lady!

Hel. I hope, sir, I have your good will to 16
have mine own good fortune.

Par. You had my prayers to lead them on;
and to keep them on, have them still. O! my
knave, how does my old lady?   20

Clo. So that you had her wrinkles, and I her
money, I would she did as you say.

Par. Why, I say nothing.

Clo. Marry, you are the wiser man; for many 24
a man's tongue shakes out his master's undoing.
To say nothing, to do nothing, to know nothing,
and to have nothing, is to be a great part of your
title; which is within a very little of nothing.   28

Par. Away! [Before God,] th'art a knave.

Clo. You should have said, sir, before a knave
thou'rt a knave; that is, before me thou'rt a
knave: this had been truth, sir.   32

Par. Go to, thou art a witty fool; I have
found thee.

Clo. Did you find me in yourself, sir? or were
you taught to find me? The search, sir, was 36
profitable; and much fool may you find in you,
even to the world's pleasure and the increase of
laughter.

Par. A good knave, i'faith, and well fed.   40
Madam, my lord will go away to-night;
A very serious business calls on him.
The great prerogative and rite of love,

28 title: *value*
35 in yourself: *by yourself (used punningly)*

Which, as your due, time claims, he does acknowl-
    edge,   44
But puts it off to a compell'd restraint;
Whose want, and whose delay, is strew'd with sweets,
Which they distil now in the curbed time,
To make the coming hour o'erflow with joy,   48
And pleasure drown the brim.

    Hel.   What's his will else?

   Par. That you will take your instant leave o' the
    king,
And make this haste as your own good proceeding,
Strengthen'd with what apology you think   52
May make it probable need.

    Hel.   What more commands he?

   Par. That, having this obtain'd, you presently
Attend his further pleasure.

    Hel. In everything I wait upon his will.   56

    Par. I shall report it so.   *Exit Parolles.*

    Hel. [*To Clown.*]   I pray you come, sirrah.

                    Exit [*followed by Clown*].

Scene Five

[*Another Room in the Same*]

Enter Lafeu and Bertram.

   Laf. But I hope your lordship thinks not
him a soldier.

   Ber. Yes, my lord, and of very valiant approof.

   Laf. You have it from his own deliverance.   4

45 *Postpones it because of an unavoidable necessity*
47 curbed time: *time of restraint*
51 *And make this haste appear to arise from your own desires*
53 make . . . need: *make the necessity plausible*
54 this: *i.e. permission to depart*   presently: *at once*
3 very . . . approof: *proved valor*

Ber. And by other warranted testimony.

Laf. Then my dial goes not true: I took this
lark for a bunting.

Ber. I do assure you, my lord, he is very 8
great in knowledge, and accordingly valiant.

Laf. I have then sinned against his experience
and transgressed against his valour; and my
state that way is dangerous, since I cannot yet 12
find in my heart to repent. Here he comes; I
pray you, make us friends; I will pursue the
amity.

Enter Parolles.

Par. [*To Bertram.*] These things shall be 16
done, sir.

Laf. Pray you, sir, who's his tailor?

Par. Sir?

Laf. O! I know him well, I, sir. He, sir, 's 20
a good workman, a very good tailor.

Ber. [*Aside to Parolles.*] Is she gone to the
king?

Par. She is.   24

Ber. Will she away to-night?

Par. As you'll have her.

Ber. I have writ my letters, casketed my treasure,
Given orders for our horses, and to-night,   28
When I should take possession of the bride,
End ere I do begin.

Laf. A good traveller is something at the latter end of a dinner; but one that lies three 32
thirds, and uses a known truth to pass a thousand nothings with, should be once heard and
thrice beaten. God save you, captain.

6 my . . . true: *I am mistaken*
9 accordingly: *to a corresponding degree*   14 pursue: *further*

Ber. Is there any unkindness between my 36
lord and you, monsieur?

Par. I know not how I have deserved to run
into my lord's displeasure.

Laf. You have made shift to run into 't, boots 40
and spurs and all, like him that leaped into the
custard; and out of it you'll run again, rather
than suffer question for your residence.

Ber. It may be you have mistaken him, my 44
lord.

Laf. And shall do so ever, though I took him
at 's prayers. Fare you well, my lord; and
believe this of me, there can be no kernel in this 48
light nut; the soul of this man is his clothes.
Trust him not in matter of heavy consequence;
I have kept of them tame, and know their na-
tures. Farewell, monsieur: I have spoken better 52
of you than you have or will to deserve at my
hand; but we must do good against evil.   [*Exit.*]

Par. An idle lord, I swear.

Ber. I think [not] so.   56

Par. Why, do you not know him?

Ber. Yes, I do know him well; and common speech
Gives him a worthy pass. Here comes my clog.

Enter Helena [followed by Clown].

Hel. I have, sir, as I was commanded from you,   60
Spoke with the king, and have procur'd his leave
For present parting; only, he desires
Some private speech with you.

Ber.   I shall obey his will.

38, 39 run into: *incur*   41, 42 like . . . custard; *cf. n.*
43 suffer . . . residence: *bear being questioned for your presence there*
46 do so: *i.e. take him amiss (pun on 'mistake')*
51 of them: *some of (such creatures)*
59 pass: *reputation*   62 present parting: *immediate departure*

You must not marvel, Helen, at my course,   64
Which holds not colour with the time, nor does
The ministration and required office
On my particular: prepar'd I was not
For such a business; therefore am I found   68
So much unsettled.   This drives me to entreat you
That presently you take your way for home;
And rather muse than ask why I entreat you;
For my respects are better than they seem,   72
And my appointments have in them a need
Greater than shows itself at the first view
To you that know them not.   This to my mother.
                                   [*Giving a letter.*]
'Twill be two days ere I shall see you, so   76
I leave you to your wisdom.
    Hel.   Sir, I can nothing say,
But that I am your most obedient servant.
    Ber. Come, come, no more of that.
    Hel.   And ever shall
With true observance seek to eke out that   80
Wherein toward me my homely stars have fail'd
To equal my great fortune.
    Ber.   Let that go:
My haste is very great.   Farewell: hie home.
    Hel. Pray sir, your pardon.
    Ber.   Well, what would you say? 84
    Hel. I am not worthy of the wealth I owe,
Nor dare I say 'tis mine, and yet it is;
But, like a timorous thief, most fain would steal
What law does vouch mine own.
    Ber.   What would you have? 88

65 holds . . . with: *does not seem suitable to*
67 particular: *part*   71 muse: *wonder*   72 respects: *motives*
73 appointments: *commands*   need: *necessity*

Hel. Something, and scarce so much: nothing, in-
deed.
I would not tell you what I would, my lord:—
Faith, yes;
Strangers and foes do sunder, and not kiss.   92

    Ber. I pray you, stay not, but in haste to horse.

    Hel. I shall not break your bidding, good my lord.
[*To Clown.*] Where are my other men? [*To Parolles.*]
    Monsieur, farewell.   *Exit.*

    Ber. Go thou toward home; where I will never
    come   96
Whilst I can shake my sword or hear the drum.
Away! and for our flight.
  Par.   Bravely, *coragio!*
                              [*Exeunt.*]

ACT THIRD

Scene One

[*Florence. A Room in the Duke's Palace*]

*Flourish. Enter the Duke of Florence [and] the
    two Frenchmen [the Lords], with a troop of sol-
    diers.*

    Duke. So that from point to point now have you
    heard
The fundamental reasons of this war,
Whose great decision hath much blood let forth,
And more thirsts after.

    1. Lord.   Holy seems the quarrel   4
Upon your Grace's part; black and fearful
On the opposer.

94 break: *disobey*   98 coragio: *courage*
3 decision: *act of deciding*

Duke. Therefore we marvel much our cousin France
Would in so just a business shut his bosom   8
Against our borrowing prayers.

1. Lord.   Good my lord,
The reasons of our state I cannot yield,
But like a common and an outward man,
That the great figure of a council frames   12
By self-unable motion: therefore dare not
Say what I think of it, since I have found
Myself in my incertain grounds to fail
As often as I guess'd.

Duke.   Be it his pleasure.   16

2. Lord. But I am sure the younger of our nature,
That surfeit on their ease, will day by day
Come here for physic.

Duke.   Welcome shall they be,
And all the honours that can fly from us   20
Shall on them settle. You know your places well;
When better fall, for your avails they fell.
To-morrow to the field.   *Flourish. [Exeunt.]*

Scene Two

[Rousillon. A Room in the Countess's Palace]

Enter Countess and Clown.

Count. It hath happened all as I would have
had it, save that he comes not along with her.

Clo. By my troth, I take my young lord to be
a very melancholy man.   4

10 yield: *tell*
11 But like: *except as*   outward: *having no access to councils of state*
12, 13 That . . . motion; *cf. n.*
16 Be . . . pleasure: *let us suppose it his will*
22 better fall: *better places fall vacant*   for your avails: *to your
    advantage*

Count. By what observance, I pray you?

Clo. Why, he will look upon his boot and sing; mend the ruff and sing; ask questions and sing; pick his teeth and sing. I know a man 8 that had this trick of melancholy hold a goodly manor for a song.

Count. [*Opening a letter.*] Let me see what he writes, and when he means to come.   12

Clo. I have no mind to Isbel since I was at court. Our old lings and our Isbels o' the country are nothing like your old ling and your Isbels o' the court: the brains of my Cupid's knocked 16 out, and I begin to love, as an old man loves money, with no stomach.

Count. What have we here?

Clo. E'en that you have there.   *Exit.* 20

[*Countess reads*] *a Letter.* 'I have sent you a daughter-in-law: she hath recovered the king, and undone me. I have wedded her, not bedded her; and sworn to make the "not" eternal. You shall 24 hear I am run away: know it before the report come. If there be breadth enough in the world, I will hold a long distance. My duty to you.

Your unfortunate son,   28

Bertram.'

This is not well, rash and unbridled boy,
To fly the favours of so good a king!
To pluck his indignation on thy head   **32**
By the misprising of a maid too virtuous
For the contempt of empire!

5 observance: *observation*   9, 10 hold . . . for: *value . . . at*
14 lings: *a kind of fish*   22 recovered: *healed*
27 hold: *keep*   32 pluck: *bring down*
33 misprising: *despising*   34 *For even an emperor to look down upon*

[Re-]enter Clown.

Clo. O madam! yonder is heavy news within
between two soldiers and my young lady.   36
Count. What is the matter?
Clo. Nay, there is some comfort in the news,
some comfort; your son will not be killed so
soon as I thought he would.   40
Count. Why should he be killed?
Clo. So say I, madam, if he run away, as I
hear he does: the danger is in standing to 't;
that's the loss of men, though it be the getting 44
of children. Here they come will tell you more;
for my part, I only hear your son was run away.
                                                [Exit.]

Enter Helen and two Gentlemen [the French Lords].

1. Gen. Save you, good madam.
Hel. Madam, my lord is gone, for ever gone.   48
2. Gen. Do not say so.
Count. Think upon patience. Pray you, gentlemen,
I have felt so many quirks of joy and grief,
That the first face of neither, on the start,   52
Can woman me unto 't. Where is my son, I pray you?
2. Gen. Madam, be's gone to serve the Duke of
        Florence:
We met him thitherward; for thence we came,
And, after some dispatch in hand at court,   56
Thither we bend again.
Hel. Look on his letter, madam; here's my passport.
'When thou canst get the ring upon my finger,
which never shall come off, and show me a child 60
begotten of thy body that I am father to, then

52 on the start: *on sudden appearance*
53 woman me unto 't: *make me show a woman's emotions*
55 thitherward: *on his way thither*   56 dispatch: *business*

    call me husband: but in such a "then" I write
a "never." '
This is a dreadful sentence.   64
    Count. Brought you this letter, gentlemen?
    1. Gen.   Ay, madam;
And for the contents' sake are sorry for our pains.
    Count. I prithee, lady, have a better cheer;
If thou engrossest all the griefs are thine,   68
Thou robb'st me of a moiety: he was my son,
But I do wash his name out of my blood,
And thou art all my child.   Towards Florence is he?
    2. Gen. Ay, madam.
    Count.   And to be a soldier?   72
    2. Gen. Such is his noble purpose; and, believe 't,
The duke will lay upon him all the honour
That good convenience claims.
    Count.   Return you thither?
    1. Gen. Ay, madam, with the swiftest wing of
    speed.   76
    Hel. 'Till I have no wife, I have nothing in France.'
'Tis bitter.
    Count.   Find you that there?
    Hel.   Ay, madam.
    1. Gen. 'Tis but the boldness of his hand,
haply, which his heart was not consenting to.   80
    Count. Nothing in France until he have no wife!
There's nothing here that is too good for him
But only she; and she deserves a lord
That twenty such rude boys might tend upon,   84
And call her hourly mistress.   Who was with him?
    1. Gen. A servant only, and a gentleman
Which ī have some time known.

67 cheer: *countenance*
68 *If you take exclusive possession of all the sorrows that are yours*
69 moiety: *half*   75 good convenience claims: *propriety permits*

Count.   Parolles, was it not?

1. Gen. Ay, my good lady, he.   88

Count. A very tainted fellow, and full of wickedness.
My son corrupts a well-derived nature
With his inducement.

    1. Gen.   Indeed, good lady,
The fellow has a deal of that too much,   92
Which holds him much to have.

    Count. Y'are welcome, gentlemen.
I will entreat you, when you see my son,
To tell him that his sword can never win   96
The honour that he loses: more I'll entreat you
Written to bear along.

    2. Gen.   We serve you, madam,
In that and all your worthiest affairs.

    Count. Not so, but as we change our courtesies.   100
Will you draw near?

                    Exit [*with the two Gentlemen*].

    Hel. 'Till I have no wife, I have nothing in France.'
Nothing in France until he has no wife!
Thou shalt have none, Rousillon, none in France;   104
Then hast thou all again. Poor lord! is 't I
That chase thee from thy country, and expose
Those tender limbs of thine to the event
Of the none-sparing war? and is it I   108
That drive thee from the sportive court, where thou
Wast shot at with fair eyes, to be the mark
Of smoky muskets? O you leaden messengers,
That ride upon the violent speed of fire,   112
Fly with false aim; move the still-pairing air,
That sings with piercing; do not touch my lord!

90 well-derived nature: *excellent natural disposition*
91 With his inducement: *through his influence*
92, 93 *Cf. n.*   99 worthiest: *most worthy*
100 *You are my servants only in the language of compliment*
107 event: *consequence*   113 still-pairing: *ever reuniting*

Whoever shoots at him, I set him there;
Whoever charges on his forward breast,   **116**
I am the caitiff that do hold him to 't;
And, though I kill him not, I am the cause
His death was so effected: better 'twere
I met the ravin lion when he roar'd   **120**
With sharp constraint of hunger; better 'twere
That all the miseries which nature owes
Were mine at once.   No, come thou home, Rousillon,
Whence honour but of danger wins a scar,   **124**
As oft it loses all: I will be gone;
My being here it is that holds thee hence:
Shall I stay here to do 't? no, no, although
The air of paradise did fan the house,   **128**
And angels offic'd all: I will be gone,
That pitiful rumour may report my flight,
To consolate thine ear.   Come, night; end, day!
For with the dark, poor thief, I'll steal away.   **132**
                                                   Exit.

Scene Three

[*Florence.   Before the Duke's Palace*]

Flourish.   Enter the Duke of Florence, Rousillon,
drum and trumpets, Soldiers, Parolles.

 Duke. The general of our horse thou art; and we,
Great in our hope, lay our best love and credence
Upon thy promising fortune.
 Ber.   Sir, it is
A charge too heavy for my strength, but yet   **4**
We'll strive to bear it for your worthy sake

120 ravin: *ravenous*
124 but . . . scar: *wins nothing except a scar from danger*
129 offic'd all: *did all the duties of the household*
130 pitiful: *compassionate*   131 consolate: *console*

To th' extreme edge of hazard.
 Duke.   Then go thou forth,
And fortune play upon thy prosperous helm
As thy auspicious mistress!
 Ber.   This very day, 8
Great Mars, I put myself into thy file:
Make me but like my thoughts, and I shall prove
A lover of thy drum, hater of love. *Exeunt omnes.*

Scene Four

[Rousillon.　A Room in the Countess's Palace]

Enter Countess and Steward.

 Count. Alas! and would you take the letter of her?
Might you not know she would do as she has done,
By sending me a letter? Read it again.

[Steward reads a] Letter. 'I am Saint Jaques' pilgrim,
  thither gone: 4
 Ambitious love hath so in me offended
That bare-foot plod I the cold ground upon
 With sainted vow my faults to have amended.
Write, write, that from the bloody course of war, 8
 My dearest master, your dear son, may hie:
Bless him at home in peace, whilst I from far
 His name with zealous fervour sanctify:
His taken labours bid him me forgive; 12
 I, his despiteful Juno, sent him forth
From courtly friends, with camping foes to live,
 Where death and danger dogs the heels of worth:

9 into thy file: *in your ranks*   4 Saint Jaques' pilgrim; *cf. n.*
11 sanctify: *adore*
12 His taken labours: *the labors he has experienced*
13 despiteful Juno; *cf. n.*

He is too good and fair for Death and me;   16
Whom I myself embrace, to set him free.'
    Count. Ah, what sharp stings are in her mildest
      words!
Rinaldo, you did never lack advice so much,
As letting her pass so: had I spoke with her,   20
I could have well diverted her intents,
Which thus she hath prevented.
    Stew.   Pardon me, madam:
If I had given you this at over-night,
She might have been o'erta'en; and yet she writes,   24
Pursuit would be but vain.
    Count.   What angel shall
Bless this unworthy husband? he cannot thrive,
Unless her prayers, whom heaven delights to hear,
And loves to grant, reprieve him from the wrath   28
Of greatest justice. Write, write, Rinaldo,
To this unworthy husband of his wife.
Let every word weigh heavy of her worth
That he does weigh too light: my greatest grief,   32
Though little he do feel it, set down sharply.
Dispatch the most convenient messenger:
When haply he shall hear that she is gone,
He will return; and hope I may that she,   36
Hearing so much, will speed her foot again,
Led hither by pure love. Which of them both
Is dearest to me I have no skill in sense
To make distinction. Provide this messenger.   40
My heart is heavy and mine age is weak;
Grief would have tears, and sorrow bids me speak.
                                      Exeunt.

---

17 Whom: *i.e. Death*   **19** did . . . much: *were never so ill-advised*
20 As: *as you were in*   **23** at over-night: *last evening*
31 weigh heavy of: *emphasize*
39 I . . . sense: *my senses are not skilled enough*

Scene Five

[Without the Walls of Florence]

*A tucket afar off.   Enter old Widow of Florence, her
daughter [Diana], Violenta and Mariana, with
other Citizens.*

Wid. Nay, come; for if they do approach the
city, we shall lose all the sight.

Dia. They say the French count has done
most honourable service.   4

Wid. It is reported that he has taken their
greatest commander, and that with his own
hand he slew the duke's brother. We have lost
our labour; they are gone a contrary way: 8
hark! you may know by their trumpets.

Mar. Come; let's return again, and suffice
ourselves with the report of it. Well, Diana, take
heed of this French earl: the honour of a maid 12
is her name, and no legacy is so rich as honesty.

Wid. I have told my neighbour how you have
been solicited by a gentleman his companion.

Mar. I know that knave, hang him! one 16
Parolles: a filthy officer he is in those suggestions
for the young earl. Beware of them, Diana;
their promises, enticements, oaths, tokens, and
all these engines of lust, are not the things they 20
go under: many a maid hath been seduced by
them; and the misery is, example, that so terrible
shows in the wrack of maidenhood, cannot for all
that dissuade succession, but that they are limed 24
with the twigs that threatens them. I hope I

Scene Five S.d. tucket: *trumpet-call*   Violenta; *cf. n.*
17, 18 suggestions for: *allurements in behalf of*
21 go under: *pretend to be*   23 shows: *appears*
24 dissuade succession: *prevent recurrence*   limed: *ensnared*

need not to advise you further; but I hope your
own grace will keep you where you are, though
there were no further danger known but the 28
modesty which is so lost.

Dia. You shall not need to fear me.

Wid. I hope so.

      Enter Helen [in the dress of a Pilgrim].

              Look, here comes a pilgrim:
I know she will lie at my house; thither they 32
send one another.   I'll question her.

God save you, pilgrim! whither are [you] bound?

Hel. To Saint Jaques le Grand.

Where do the palmers lodge, I do beseech you?   36

Wid. At the Saint Francis, here beside the port.

Hel. Is this the way?

Wid.   Ay, marry, is 't.

                    A march afar.
                    Hark you!

They come this way.   If you will tarry, holy pilgrim,
But till the troops come by,   40
I will conduct you where you shall be lodg'd:
The rather, for I think I know your hostess
As ample as myself.

Hel.   Is it yourself?

Wid. If you shall please so, pilgrim.   44

Hel. I thank you, and will stay upon your leisure.

Wid. You came, I think, from France?

Hel.   I did so.

Wid. Here you shall see a countryman of yours
That has done worthy service.

Hel.   His name, I pray you. 48

Dia. The Count Rousillon: know you such a one?

30 fear me: *have fears for me*   37 port: *gate*
43 ample: *well*   45 stay upon: *await*

Hel. But by the ear, that hears most nobly of him;
His face I know not.

Dia.   Whatsome'er he is,
He's bravely taken here.   He stole from France,   52
As 'tis reported: for the king had married him
Against his liking.   Think you it is so?

Hel. Ay, surely, mere the truth: I know his lady.

Dia. There is a gentleman that serves the count   56
Reports but coarsely of her.

Hel.   What's his name?

Dia. Monsieur Parolles.

Hel.   O, I believe with him.
In argument of praise, or to the worth
Of the great count himself, she is too mean   60
To have her name repeated: all her deserving
Is a reserved honesty, and that
I have not heard examin'd.

Dia.   Alas, poor lady!
'Tis a hard bondage to become the wife   64
Of a detesting lord.

Wid. I write, good creature, wheresoe'er she is,
Her heart weighs sadly.   This young maid might do
      her
A shrewd turn if she pleas'd.

Hel.   How do you mean? 68
May be the amorous count solicits her
In the unlawful purpose.

Wid.   He does, indeed;
And brokes with all that can in such a suit
Corrupt the tender honour of a maid: 72

50 by the ear: *by hearsay*   51 Whatsome'er: *whatever*
55 mere the truth: *the simple truth*
59 In . . . praise: *as a subject of formal laudation*   to the worth:
      compared with the worth   60 mean: *humble*
62 honesty: *chastity*   63 examin'd: *questioned*
66 write: *warrant*   68 shrewd: *evil*
71 brokes with: *traffics in*

But she is arm'd for him and keeps her guard
In honestest defence.

> *Drum and colours. Enter Count Rousillon,*
> *Parolles, and the whole army.*

 Mar.   The gods forbid else!
 Wid. So, now they come.
That is Antonio, the duke's eldest son;   **76**
That, Escalus.
 Hel.   Which is the Frenchman?
 Dia.   He;
That with the plume: 'tis a most gallant fellow;
I would he lov'd his wife: if he were honester,
He were much goodlier. Is 't not a handsome gentle-
  man?   **80**
 Hel. I like him well.
 Dia. 'Tis pity he is not honest. Yond's that same
  knave
That leads him to these places: were I his lady,
I would poison that vile rascal.
 Hel.   Which is he? **84**
 Dia. That jackanapes with scarfs. Why is he
  melancholy?
 Hel. Perchance he's hurt i' the battle.
 Par. Lose our drum! well.   **88**
 Mar. He's shrewdly vexed at something.
Look, he has spied us.
 Wid. Marry, hang you!
 Mar. And your courtesy, for a ring-carrier! **92**
   Exit [Bertram, with Parolles and the army].
 Wid. The troop is past. Come, pilgrim, I will bring
  you

74 forbid else: *forbid it should be otherwise* **82** Yond's: *yonder's*
89 shrewdly: *keenly*   **92** ring-carrier: *go-between*

Where you shall host: of enjoin'd penitents
There's four or five, to great Saint Jaques bound,
Already at my house.

   Hel.   I humbly thank you.   96
Please it this matron and this gentle maid
To eat with us to-night, the charge and thanking
Shall be for me; and, to requite you further,
I will bestow some precepts of this virgin   100
Worthy the note.

   Both.   We'll take your offer kindly.

                                      Exeunt.

Scene Six

[*Camp before Florence*]

*Enter Count Rousillon and the Frenchmen [the
Lords], as at first.*

   1. Lord. Nay, good my lord, put him
to 't: let him have his way.

   2. Lord. If your lordship find him not a
hilding, hold me no more in your respect.   **4**

   1. Lord. On my life, my lord, a bubble.

   Ber. Do you think I am so far deceived in him?

   1. Lord. Believe it, my lord, in mine own
direct knowledge, without any malice, but to **8**
speak of him as my kinsman, he's a most notable
coward, an infinite and endless liar, an hourly
promise-breaker, the owner of no one good quality
worthy your lordship's entertainment.   **12**

   2. Lord. It were fit you knew him, lest, re-

94 host: *lodge*   enjoin'd penitents: *pilgrims performing imposed
penances*   **100** bestow . . . of: *give some advice to*
101 Worthy the note: *worth noting*   **2** to 't: *to the test*
4 hilding: *coward*   **5** bubble: *sham*
12 entertainment: *maintaining*

posing too far in his virtue, which he hath not,
he might at some great and trusty business in a
main danger fail you.   16

Ber. I would I knew in what particular action
to try him.

2. Lord. None better than to let him fetch
off his drum, which you hear him so confidently 20
undertake to do.

1. Lord. I, with a troop of Florentines,
will suddenly surprise him: such I will have
whom I am sure he knows not from the enemy. 24
We will bind and hoodwink him so, that he shall
suppose no other but that he is carried into the
leaguer of the adversaries, when we bring him to
our own tents. Be but your lordship present at 28
his examination: if he do not, for the promise
of his life and in the highest compulsion of base
fear, offer to betray you and deliver all the intelligence in his power against you, and that 32
with the divine forfeit of his soul upon oath,
never trust my judgment in anything.

2. Lord. O, for the love of laughter, let him
fetch his drum! he says he has a stratagem 36
for 't. When your lordship sees the bottom of
his success in 't, and to what metal this counterfeit lump of ours will be melted, if you give him
not John Drum's entertainment, your inclining 40
cannot be removed.   Here he comes.

Enter Parolles.

1. Lord. O, for the love of laughter, hinder

16 main: *very great*   19, 20 fetch off: *rescue*
25 hoodwink: *blindfold*   26 no other but: *nothing else than*
27 leaguer: *camp*   30 in: *under*   highest: *strongest*
37 bottom: *extent*
40 John Drum's entertainment; *cf. n.*   inclining: *partiality*

not the honour of his design! let him fetch off
his drum in any hand.   44

Ber. How now, monsieur! this drum sticks
sorely in your disposition.

2. Lord. A pox on 't! let it go: 'tis but a
drum.   48

Par. 'But a drum!' Is 't 'but a drum'? A
drum so lost! There was excellent command, to
charge in with our horse upon our own wings,
and to rend our own soldiers!   52

2. Lord. That was not to be blamed in the
command of the service: it was a disaster of war
that Cæsar himself could not have prevented if
he had been there to command.   56

Ber. Well, we cannot greatly condemn our
success: some dishonour we had in the loss of
that drum; but it is not to be recovered.

Par. It might have been recovered.   60

Ber. It might; but it is not now.

Par. It is to be recovered. But that the
merit of service is seldom attributed to the true
and exact performer, I would have that drum or 64
another, or *hic jacet.*

Ber. Why, if you have a stomach, to 't, monsieur;
if you think your mystery in stratagem can bring
this instrument of honour again into his native 68
quarter, be magnanimous in the enterprise and
go on; I will grace the attempt for a worthy
exploit: if you speed well in it, the duke shall
both speak of it and extend to you what further 72

44 in any hand: *at all events*
54 command of the service: *commanders of the army*
65 hic jacet; *cf. n.*   66 stomach: *inclination*   to 't: *attempt it*
67 mystery: *skill*   70 grace: *honor*
71 speed: *succeed*

becomes his greatness, even to the utmost syllable of your worthiness.

Par. By the hand of a soldier, I will undertake it.   76

Ber. But you must not now slumber in it.

Par. I'll about it this evening: and I will presently pen down my dilemmas, encourage myself in my certainty, put myself into my 80 mortal preparation, and by midnight look to hear further from me.

Ber. May I be bold to acquaint his Grace you are gone about it?   84

Par. I know not what the success will be, my lord, but the attempt I vow.

Ber. I know th' art valiant, and, to the possibility of thy soldiership, will subscribe for thee. 88 Farewell.

Par. I love not many words.   *Exit.*

1. Lord. No more than a fish loves water. Is not this a strange fellow, my lord, that so con- 92 fidently seems to undertake this business, which he knows is not to be done; damns himself to do, and dares better be damned than to do 't?

2. Lord. You do not know him, my lord, as 96 we do: certain it is, that he will steal himself into a man's favour, and for a week escape a great deal of discoveries; but when you find him out you have him ever after.   100

Ber. Why, do you think he will make no deed

73, 74 utmost syllable: *last jot*   78 about: *go about*
79 pen . . . dilemmas: *write out the difficulties to be overcome*
79, 80 encourage . . . certainty: *make sure of my success*
80, 81 put . . . preparation: *prepare for the possibility of death*
87 possibility: *extent*   94 damns: *condemns*
97 steal: *insinuate*

at all of this that so seriously he does address
himself unto?

1. Lord. None in the world; but return 104
with an invention and clap upon you two or
three probable lies.   But we have almost imbost him, you shall see his fall to-night; for,
indeed, he is not for your lordship's respect.   108

2. Lord. We'll make you some sport with
the fox ere we case him.   He was first smoked
by the old Lord Lafeu: when his disguise and
he is parted, tell me what a sprat you shall find 112
him; which you shall see this very night.

1. Lord. I must go look my twigs: he
shall be caught.

Ber. Your brother he shall go along with me.   116

1. Lord. As 't please your lordship: I'll
leave you.   [*Exit.*]

Ber. Now will I lead you to the house, and show you
The lass I spoke of.

2. Lord.   But you say she's honest.   120

Ber. That's all the fault.   I spoke with her but once,
And found her wondrous cold; but I sent to her,
By this same coxcomb that we have i' the wind,
Tokens and letters which she did re-send;   124
And this is all I have done.   She's a fair creature;
Will you go see her?

2. Lord.   With all my heart, my lord.

                                                     Exeunt.

102, 103 address . . . unto: *undertake*
106 imbost: *surrounded*   105 clap: *foist*
110 case: *flay*   smoked: *found out*   108 for: *worthy of*
114 look my twigs: *see to my snares*   112 sprat: *a worthless fish*
121 all the fault: *the only drawback*
123 have . . . wind: *are in pursuit of*

Scene Seven

[*Florence.   A Room in the Widow's House*]

Enter Helen and Widow.

Hel. If you misdoubt me that I am not she,
I know not how I shall assure you further,
But I shall lose the grounds I work upon.

Wid. Though my estate be fall'n, I was well born,   4
Nothing acquainted with these businesses;
And would not put my reputation now
In any staining act.

Hel.   Nor would I wish you.
First, give me trust, the count he is my husband,   8
And what to your sworn counsel I have spoken
Is so from word to word; and then you cannot,
By the good aid that I of you shall borrow,
Err in bestowing it.

Wid.   I should believe you: 12
For you have show'd me that which well approves
Y'are great in fortune.

Hel.   Take this purse of gold,
And let me buy your friendly help thus far,
Which I will over-pay and pay again   16
When I have found it.   The count he woos your daugh-
     ter,
Lays down his wanton siege before her beauty,
Resolv'd to carry her: let her in fine consent,
As we'll direct her how 'tis best to bear it.   20
Now, his important blood will nought deny

3 *Cf. n.*   5 Nothing acquainted: *entirely unfamiliar*
6, 7 put . . . act: *do anything tending to injure my reputation*
9 to . . . counsel: *to you in sworn secrecy*
10 from word to word: *every word*   13 approves: *proves*
19 carry: *conquer*   in fine: *in short*
20 bear it: *conduct the affair*   21 important: *importunate*

That she'll demand: a ring the county wears,
That downward hath succeeded in his house
From son to son, some four or five descents   24
Since the first father wore it: this ring he holds
In most rich choice; yet, in his idle fire,
To buy his will, it would not seem too dear,
Howe'er repented after.

    Wid.   Now I see   28
The bottom of your purpose.

    Hel. You see it lawful then. It is no more,
But that your daughter, ere she seems as won,
Desires this ring, appoints him an encounter,   32
In fine, delivers me to fill the time,
Herself most chastely absent. After,
To marry her, I'll add three thousand crowns
To what is past already.

    Wid.   I have yielded.   36
Instruct my daughter how she shall persever,
That time and place with this deceit so lawful
May prove coherent. Every night he comes
With musics of all sorts and songs compos'd   40
To her unworthiness: it nothing steads us
To chide him from our eaves, for he persists
As if his life lay on 't.

    Hel.   Why then to-night
Let us assay our plot; which, if it speed,   44
Is wicked meaning in a lawful deed,
And lawful meaning in a lawful act,
Where both not sin, and yet a sinful fact.
But let's about it.   *[Exeunt.]* 48

22 county: *count*
26 rich choice: *high estimation*   idle fire: *foolish passion*
37 persever: *proceed*   39 prove coherent: *agree*
41 steads: *avails*   44 assay: *try*

ACT FOURTH

Scene One

[Without the Florentine Camp]

Enter one of the Frenchmen [First Lord] with
five or six other Soldiers in ambush.

1. Lord. He can come no other way but
by this hedge-corner. When you sally upon
him, speak what terrible language you will:
though you understand it not yourselves, no 4
matter; for we must not seem to understand
him, unless some one among us, whom we must
produce for an interpreter.

1. Sold. Good captain, let me be the in- 8
terpreter.

1. Lord. Art not acquainted with him?
knows he not thy voice?

1. Sold. No, sir, I warrant you.   12

1. Lord. But what linsey-woolsey hast
thou to speak to us again?

1. Sold. E'en such as you speak to me.

1. Lord. He must think us some band of 16
strangers i' th' adversary's entertainment. Now,
he hath a smack of all neighbouring languages;
therefore we must every one be a man of his
own fancy, not to know what we speak one to 20
another; so we seem to know, is to know
straight our purpose: chough's language, gabble
enough, and good enough. As for you, interpreter, you must seem very politic. But couch, ho! 24

13 linsey-woolsey: *nondescript (language)*
17 strangers: *foreigners*
22 straight: *immediately*   chough's: *crow's*   24 couch: *hide*

here he comes, to beguile two hours in a sleep,
and then to return and swear the lies he forges.

Enter Parolles.

Par. Ten o'clock: within these three hours
'twill be time enough to go home. What shall 28
I say I have done? It must be a very plausive
invention that carries it. They begin to smoke
me, and disgraces have of late knocked too often
at my door. I find my tongue is too foolhardy; but 32
my heart hath the fear of Mars before it and of
his creatures, not daring the reports of my tongue.

1. Lord. [*Aside.*] This is the first truth that e'er
thine own tongue was guilty of.   36

Par. What the devil should move me to undertake the recovery of this drum, being not ignorant of the impossibility, and knowing I had
no such purpose? I must give myself some hurts 40
and say I got them in exploit. Yet slight ones
will not carry it: they will say, 'Came you off
with so little?' and great ones I dare not give.
Wherefore, what's the instance? Tongue, I must 44
put you into a butter-woman's mouth, and buy
myself another of Bajazet's mule, if you prattle
me into these perils.

1. Lord. Is it possible he should know 48
what he is, and be that he is?

Par. I would the cutting of my garments
would serve the turn, or the breaking of my
Spanish sword.   52

1. Lord. We cannot afford you so.

Par. Or the baring of my beard, and to say
it was in stratagem.

29 plausive: *plausible*   30 carries it: *succeeds*
44 instance: *proof*   46 Bajazet's mule; *cf. n.*
53 afford you so: *let you off so cheaply*
54 baring: *shaving*

    1. Lord. 'Twould not do.   56

    Par. Or to drown my clothes, and say I was stripped.

    1. Lord. Hardly serve.

    Par. Though I swore I leapt from the 60 window of the citadel—

    1. Lord. How deep?

    Par. Thirty fathom.

    1. Lord. Three great oaths would scarce 64 make that be believed.

    Par. I would I had any drum of the enemy's: I would swear I recovered it.

    1. Lord. You shall hear one anon.   68

    Par. A drum now of the enemy's!

                         Alarum within.

1. Lord. Throca movousus, cargo, caryo, cargo.

All. Cargo, cargo, cargo, villianda par corbo, cargo.
                [They seize and blindfold him.]

    Par. O! ransom, ransom! Do not hide mine eyes. 72

Inter. Boskos thromuldo boskos.

    Par. I know you are the Muskos' regiment;
And I shall lose my life for want of language.
If there be here German, or Dane, low Dutch,   76
Italian, or French, let him speak to me:
I'll discover that which shall undo
The Florentine.

Inter.   *Boskos vauvado:*
I understand thee, and can speak thy tongue: 80
Kerelybonto, sir,
Betake thee to thy faith, for seventeen poniards
Are at thy bosom.

    Par.   O!

    Inter.   O! pray, pray, pray.

69 S.d. Alarum: *trumpet blast*   82 faith: *religion*

Manka revania dulche.

    1. Lord.   *Oscorbidulchos volivorco.* 84

    Inter. The general is content to spare thee yet,
And, hoodwink'd as thou art, will lead thee on
To gather from thee: haply thou may'st inform
Something to save thy life.

    Par.   O! let me live, 88
And all the secrets of our camp I'll show,
Their force, their purposes; nay, I'll speak that
Which you will wonder at.

    Inter.   But wilt thou faithfully?

    Par. If I do not, damn me.

    Inter.   *Acordo linta.* 92
Come on; thou art granted space.

                        Exit [*with Parolles guarded*].
                        A short alarum within.

    1. Lord. Go, tell the Count Rousillon and my brother
We have caught the woodcock, and will keep him muffled
Till we do hear from them.

    Sold.   Captain, I will. 96

    1. Lord. A' will betray us all unto ourselves:
Inform on that.

    Sold.   So I will, sir.   [*Exit.*]

    1. Lord. Till then, I'll keep him dark and safely lock'd.   *Exit.*

87 gather: *obtain information*   **93** space: *a reprieve*
95 woodcock: *fool*   muffled: *blindfolded*   **98** Inform on: *relate*

Scene Two

[Florence.   A Room in the Widow's House]

Enter Bertram and the maid called Diana.

Ber. They told me that your name was Fontibell.
Dia. No, my good lord, Diana.
Ber.   Titled goddess;
And worth it, with addition!   But, fair soul,
In your fine frame hath love no quality?   4
If the quick fire of youth light not your mind,
You are no maiden, but a monument:
When you are dead, you should be such a one
As you are now, for you are cold and stern;   8
And now you should be as your mother was
When your sweet self was got.
     Dia. She then was honest.
     Ber.   So should you be.
     Dia.   No:
My mother did but duty; such, my lord,   12
As you owe to your wife.
     Ber.   No more o' that!
I prithee do not strive against my vows.
I was compell'd to her; but I love thee
By love's own sweet constraint, and will for ever 16
Do thee all rights of service.
     Dia.   Ay, so you serve us
Till we serve you; but when you have our roses,
You barely leave our thorns to prick ourselves
And mock us with our bareness.
     Ber.   How have I sworn! 20
     Dia. 'Tis not the many oaths that makes the truth,
But the plain single vow that is vow'd true.

3 addition: *a higher title of honor*   4 quality: *standing*
11 should: *would*   19 barely: *merely*

What is not holy, that we swear not by,
But take the high'st to witness: then, pray you, tell
    me,   24
If I should swear by Jove's great attributes
I lov'd you dearly, would you believe my oaths,
When I did love you ill? This has no holding,
To swear by him whom I protest to love,   28
That I will work against him: therefore your oaths
Are words and poor conditions, but unseal'd,
At least in my opinion.

Ber.   Change it, change it.
Be not so holy-cruel: love is holy;   32
And my integrity ne'er knew the crafts
That you do charge men with. Stand no more off,
But give thyself unto my sick desires,
Who then recovers: say thou art mine, and ever   36
My love as it begins shall so persever.

Dia. I see that men make rope's in such a scarre
That we'll forsake ourselves. Give me that ring.

Ber. I'll lend it thee, my dear; but have no power   40
To give it from me.

Dia.   Will you not, my lord?

Ber. It is an honour longing to our house,
Bequeathed down from many ancestors,
Which were the greatest obloquy i' the world   44
In me to lose.

Dia.   Mine honour's such a ring:
My chastity's the jewel of our house,
Bequeathed down from many ancestors,
Which were the greatest obloquy i' the world   48
In me to lose. Thus your own proper wisdom

25 Jove's; *cf. n.*   27 holding: *consistency*
30 conditions: *covenants*   unseal'd; *cf. n.*   33 crafts: *deceits*
36 Who then recovers: *which then recover*   38 *Cf. n.*
42 longing: *belonging*   49 proper: *own (used intensively)*

Brings in the champion honour on my part
Against your vain assault.

   Ber.   Here, take my ring:
My house, mine honour, yea, my life, be thine,   **52**
And I'll be bid by thee.

   Dia. When midnight comes, knock at my chamber-
     window:
I'll order take my mother shall not hear.
Now will I charge you in the band of truth,   **56**
When you have conquer'd my yet maiden bed,
Remain there but an hour, nor speak to me.
My reasons are most strong, and you shall know them
When back again this ring shall be deliver'd: **60**
And on your finger in the night I'll put
Another ring that, what in time proceeds,
May token to the future our past deeds.
Adieu, till then; then, fail not. You have won   **64**
A wife of me, though there my hope be done.

   Ber. A heaven on earth I have won by wooing thee.
                                        [Exit.]

   Dia. For which live long to thank both heaven and
     me!
You may so in the end.   **68**
My mother told me just how he would woo
As if she sat in's heart; she says all men
Have the like oaths: he had sworn to marry me
When his wife's dead; therefore I'll lie with him   **72**
When I am buried. Since Frenchmen are so braid,
Marry that will, I live and die a maid:
Only in this disguise I think 't no sin
To cozen him that would unjustly win.   *Exit.* **76**

50 on my part: *in my behalf*
56 band: *bond*
62 what . . . proceeds: *whatever happens in the future*
63 token: *be witness of*   73 braid: *deceitful*
76 cozen: *deceive*

Scene Three

[The Florentine Camp]

*Enter the two French Captains [the Lords] and
some two or three Soldiers.*

1. Lord. You have not given him his
mother's letter?

2. Lord. I have delivered it an hour since:
there is something in 't that stings his nature, 4
for on the reading it he changed almost into
another man.

1. Lord. He has much worthy blame laid
upon him for shaking off so good a wife and so 8
sweet a lady.

2. Lord. Especially he hath incurred the
everlasting displeasure of the king, who had
even tuned his bounty to sing happiness to him. 12
I will tell you a thing, but you shall let it dwell
darkly with you.

1. Lord. When you have spoken it, 'tis
dead, and I am the grave of it.   16

2. Lord. He hath perverted a young gentlewoman here in Florence, of a most chaste renown; and this night he fleshes his will in the
spoil of her honour: he hath given her his 20
monumental ring, and thinks himself made in
the unchaste composition.

1. Lord. Now, God delay our rebellion!
as we are ourselves, what things are we!   24

2. Lord. Merely our own traitors: and as

7 worthy: *deserved*   13, 14 dwell . . . with: *be kept secret by*
19 fleshes: *gratifies*   20 spoil: *spoliation*
21 monumental: *commemorative*   22 composition: *compact*
23 God . . . rebellion: *God make us slow to rebel*
25 our own traitors: *traitors to ourselves*

in the common course of all treasons, we still
see them reveal themselves, till they attain to
their abhorred ends, so he that in this action 28
contrives against his own nobility, in his proper
stream o'erflows himself.

1. Lord. Is it not meant damnable in us,
to be trumpeters of our unlawful intents? We 32
shall not then have his company to-night?

2. Lord. Not till after midnight, for he is
dieted to his hour.

1. Lord. That approaches apace: I would 36
gladly have him see his company anatomized,
that he might take a measure of his own judgments, wherein so curiously he had set this
counterfeit.   40

2. Lord. We will not meddle with him till
he come, for his presence must be the whip of
the other.

1. Lord. In the meantime what hear you 44
of these wars?

2. Lord. I hear there is an overture of peace.

1. Lord. Nay, I assure you, a peace concluded.   48

2. Lord. What will Count Rousillon do
then? will he travel higher, or return again into
France?

1. Lord. I perceive by this demand, you 52
are not altogether of his council.

2. Lord. Let it be forbid, sir; so should I
be a great deal of his act.

1. Lord. Sir, his wife some two months 56

28 ends: *destruction*   30 o'erflows: *drowns*
31, 32 Is . . . intents; *cf. n.*   35 dieted to: *fully occupied until*
37 company: *companion*   39 curiously: *carefully*
50 higher: *further into Italy*
55 of his act: *a partner in his actions*

since fled from his house: her pretence is a
pilgrimage to Saint Jaques le Grand; which
holy undertaking with most austere sanctimony
she accomplished; and, there residing, the 30
tenderness of her nature became as a prey to
her grief; in fine, made a groan of her last
breath, and now she sings in heaven.

2. Lord. How is this justified?   64

1. Lord. The stronger part of it by her
own letters, which makes her story true, even to
the point of her death: her death itself, which
could not be her office to say is come, was faith- 68
fully confirmed by the rector of the place.

2. Lord. Hath the count all this intelligence?

1. Lord. Ay, and the particular confirma-
tions, point from point, to the full arming of 72
the verity.

2. Lord. I am heartily sorry that he'll be
glad of this.

1. Lord. How mightily sometimes we 76
make us comforts of our losses!

2. Lord. And how mightily some other
times we drown our gain in tears! The great
dignity that his valour hath here acquired for 80
him shall at home be encountered with a shame
as ample.

1. Lord. The web of our life is of a mingled
yarn, good and ill together: our virtues would 84
be proud if our faults whipped them not; and
our crimes would despair if they were not
cherished by our virtues.

---

57 pretence: *purpose*   64 justified: *confirmed as true*
65 stronger: *greater*
72 arming: *corroboration*   69 rector: *governor*

Enter a Messenger.

How now! where's your master?   88

Mess. He met the duke in the street, sir, of
whom he hath taken a solemn leave: his lordship will next morning for France. The duke hath
offered him letters of commendations to the king. 92

2. Lord. They shall be no more than needful
there, if they were more than they can commend.

Enter Count Rousillon.

1. Lord. They cannot be too sweet for the
king's tartness. Here's his lordship now.   96
How now, my lord! is 't not after midnight?

Ber. I have to-night dispatched sixteen
businesses, a month's length apiece, by an
abstract of success: I have congied with the 100
duke, done my adieu with his nearest, buried a
wife, mourned for her, writ to my lady mother
I am returning, entertained my convoy, and between these main parcels of dispatch effected 104
many nicer needs: the last was the greatest, but
that I have not ended yet.

2. Lord. If the business be of any difficulty,
and this morning your departure hence, it re- 108
quires haste of your lordship.

Ber. I mean, the business is not ended, as
fearing to hear of it hereafter. But shall we
have this dialogue between the fool and the 112
soldier? Come, bring forth this counterfeit

93 shall: *would*
100 abstract of success: *successful summary proceeding*   congied
    with: *taken leave of*
101 done . . . nearest: *said farewell to his suite*
103 entertained: *engaged*
104 main . . . dispatch: *chief pieces of business*

module: has deceived me, like a double-
meaning prophesier.

2. Lord. Bring him forth.   116

[*Exeunt Soldiers.*]

Has sat i' the stocks all night, poor gallant
knave.

Ber. No matter; his heels have deserved it,
in usurping his spurs so long. How does he 120
carry himself?

1. Lord. I have told your lordship already,
the stocks carry him. But to answer you as you
would be understood, he weeps like a wench 124
that had shed her milk: he hath confessed himself to Morgan—whom he supposes to be a
friar—from the time of his remembrance to
this very instant disaster of his setting i' the 128
stocks: and what think you he hath confessed?

Ber. Nothing of me, has a'?

2. Lord. His confession is taken, and it
shall be read to his face: if your lordship be in 't, 132
as I believe you are, you must have the patience
to hear it.

Enter Parolles with his Interpreter [*and other
Soldiers*].

Ber. A plague upon him! muffled! he can
say nothing of me: hush! hush!   136

1. Lord. Hoodman comes! *Portotartarossa.*

Inter. He calls for the tortures: what
will you say without 'em?

Par. I will confess what I know without constraint: if ye pinch me like a pasty, I can say no
more.

114 module: *model*   120 usurping: *unworthily wearing*
128 instant: *present*

Inter. Bosko chimurcho.   144

1. Lord. Boblibindo chicurmurco.

Inter. You are a merciful general. Our general bids you answer to what I shall ask you out of a note.   148

Par. And truly, as I hope to live.

Inter. 'First, demand of him how many horse the duke is strong.' What say you to that?

Par. Five or six thousand; but very weak 152 and unserviceable: the troops are all scattered, and the commanders very poor rogues, upon my reputation and credit, and as I hope to live.

Inter. Shall I set down your answer so?   156

Par. Do: I'll take the sacrament on 't, how and which way you will.

Ber. All's one to him. What a past-saving slave is this!   160

1. Lord. Y' are deceived, my lord: this is Monsieur Parolles, the gallant militarist— that was his own phrase—that had the whole theoric of war in the knot of his scarf, and the 164 practice in the chape of his dagger.

2. Lord. I will never trust a man again for keeping his sword clean; nor believe he can have everything in him by wearing his apparel 168 neatly.

Inter. Well, that's set down.

Par. Five or six thousand horse, I said—I will say true—or thereabouts, set down, for I'll 172 speak truth.

1. Lord. He's very near the truth in this.

164 theoric: *theory*   165 chape: *the metal part of the sheath*

Ber. But I con him no thanks for 't, in the
nature he delivers it.   176

Par. Poor rogues, I pray you, say.

Inter. Well, that's set down.

Par. I humbly thank you, sir. A truth's a
truth; the rogues are marvellous poor.   180

Inter. 'Demand of him, of what strength
they are a-foot.' What say you to that?

Par. By my troth, sir, if I were to live this
present hour, I will tell true. Let me see: 184
Spurio, a hundred and fifty; Sebastian, so many;
Corambus, so many; Jaques, so many; Guiltian,
Cosmo, Lodowick, and Gratii, two hundred fifty
each; mine own company, Chitopher, Vaumond, 188
Bentii, two hundred fifty each: so that the
muster-file, rotten and sound, upon my life,
amounts not to fifteen thousand poll; half of
the which dare not shake the snow from off their 192
cassocks, lest they shake themselves to pieces.

Ber. What shall be done to him?

1. Lord. Nothing, but let him have thanks.
Demand of him my condition, and what credit 196
I have with the duke.

Inter. Well, that's set down. 'You shall
demand of him, whether one Captain Dumaine
be i' the camp, a Frenchman; what his reputa- 200
tion is with the duke; what his valour, honesty,
and expertness in wars; or whether he thinks it
were not possible, with well-weighing sums of
gold, to corrupt him to a revolt.' What say you 204
to this? what do you know of it?

Par. I beseech you, let me answer to the

175 con . . . thanks: *am not grateful to him*
175, 176 in the nature: *in view of the way in which*
183, 184 live . . . hour: *live but an hour*
193 cassocks: *military cloaks*   196 condition: *character*

particular of the inter'gatories: demand them
singly.   208

Inter. Do you know this Captain Dumaine?

Par. I know him: a' was a botcher's 'pren-
tice in Paris, from whence he was whipped for 212
getting the shrieve's fool with child; a dumb
innocent, that could not say him nay.

> [*Dumaine lifts up his hand in anger.*]

Ber. Nay, by your leave, hold your hands;
though I know his brains are forfeit to the next 216
tile that falls.

Inter. Well, is this captain in the Duke
of Florence's camp?

Par. Upon my knowledge he is, and lousy.   220

1. Lord. Nay, look not so upon me; we
shall hear of your lordship anon.

Inter. What is his reputation with the
duke?   224

Par. The duke knows him for no other but a
poor officer of mine, and writ to me this other
day to turn him out o' the band: I think I have
his letter in my pocket.   228

Inter. Marry, we'll search.

Par. In good sadness, I do not know: either
it is there, or it is upon a file with the duke's
other letters in my tent.   232

Inter. Here 'tis; here's a paper; shall I
read it to you?

Par. I do not know if it be it or no.

Ber. Our interpreter does it well.   236

---

207 particular: *detail*   211 botcher's: *mending tailor's*
213 shrieve's fool: *feeble-minded girl under the sheriff's guardianship*
230 good sadness: *all seriousness*

1. Lord. Excellently.

Inter. 'Dian, the count's a fool, and full of gold—'

Par. That is not the duke's letter, sir; that is an advertisement to a proper maid in Flo- 240 rence, one Diana, to take heed of the allurement of one Count Rousillon, a foolish idle boy, but for all that very ruttish. I pray you, sir, put it up again.   244

Inter. Nay, I'll read it first, by your favour.

Par. My meaning in 't, I protest, was very honest in the behalf of the maid; for I knew 248 the young count to be a dangerous and lascivious boy, who is a whale to virginity, and devours up all the fry it finds.

Ber. Damnable both-sides rogue!   252

Inter. 'When he swears oaths, bid him drop gold,
       and take it;

After he scores, he never pays the score:

Half won is match well made; match, and well make it;

He ne'er pays after-debts; take it before,   256

And say a soldier, Dian, told thee this:

Men are to mell with, boys are not to kiss;

For count of this, the count's a fool, I know it,

Who pays before, but not when he does owe it.   260

       Thine, as he vow'd to thee in thine ear,

                                        Parolles.'

Ber. He shall be whipped through the army with this rime in's forehead.   264

1. Lord. This is your devoted friend, sir, the manifold linguist and the armipotent soldier.

---

240 advertisement: *admonition*   243 ruttish: *lascivious*
251 fry: *young fish*   254 scores: *incurs a debt*   255 Cf. n.
258 mell: *deal*   264 in's: *on his*   266 armipotent: *powerful in arms*

Ber. I could endure anything before but a 268
cat, and now he's a cat to me.

Inter. I perceive, sir, by our general's
looks, we shall be fain to hang you.

Par. My life, sir, in any case! not that I am 272
afraid to die, but that, my offences being many,
I would repent out the remainder of nature.
Let me live, sir, in a dungeon, i' the stocks, or
anywhere, so I may live.   276

Inter. We'll see what may be done, so
you confess freely: therefore, once more to this
Captain Dumaine. You have answered to his
reputation with the duke and to his valour: 280
what is his honesty?

Par. He will steal, sir, an egg out of a cloister;
for rapes and ravishments he parallels Nessus;
he professes not keeping of oaths; in breaking 284
'em he is stronger than Hercules; he will lie,
sir, with such volubility, that you would think
truth were a fool; drunkenness is his best virtue,
for he will be swine-drunk, and in his sleep he 288
does little harm, save to his bed-clothes about
him; but they know his conditions, and lay him
in straw. I have but little more to say, sir, of his
honesty: he has everything that an honest man 292
should not have; what an honest man should
have, he has nothing.

1. Lord. I begin to love him for this.

Ber. For this description of thine honesty? A 296
pox upon him for me! he's more and more a cat.

Inter. What say you to his expertness
in war?

Par. Faith, sir, has led the drum before 300

274 *I desire to spend the rest of my life in repentance*
283 Nessus; *cf. n.*   300 led: *carried*

the English tragedians—to belie him I will
not—and more of his soldiership I know not;
except, in that country, he had the honour to be
the officer at a place there called Mile-end, to 304
instruct for the doubling of files. I would do
the man what honour I can, but of this I am
not certain.

1. Lord. He hath out-villained villainy so 308
far, that the rarity redeems him.

Ber. A pox on him! he's a cat still.

Inter. His qualities being at this poor
price, I need not to ask you if gold will corrupt 312
him to revolt.

Par. Sir, for a cardecu he will sell the fee-
simple of his salvation, the inheritance of it;
and cut th' entail from all remainders, and a 316
perpetual succession for it perpetually.

Inter. What's his brother, the other
Captain Dumaine?

2. Lord. Why does he ask him of me?   320

Inter. What's he?

Par. E'en a crow o' the same nest; not altogether so great as the first in goodness, but
greater a great deal in evil. He excels his 324
brother for a coward, yet his brother is reputed
one of the best that is. In a retreat he outruns
any lackey; marry, in coming on he has the
cramp.   328

Inter. If your life be saved, will you
undertake to betray the Florentine?

Par. Ay, and the captain of his horse, Count
Rousillon.   332

311, 312 at . . . price: *of such low value*
314 cardecu: *quart d'écu, a small French coin*
314-317 sell . . . perpetually; *cf. n.*   327 coming on: *advancing*

Inter. I'll whisper with the general, and
know his pleasure.

Par. [*Aside.*] I'll no more drumming; a
plague of all drums! Only to seem to deserve 336
well, and to beguile the supposition of that
lascivious young boy the count, have I run into
this danger. Yet who would have suspected an
ambush where I was taken?   340

Inter. There is no remedy, sir, but you
must die. The general says, you, that have so
traitorously discovered the secrets of your army,
and made such pestiferous reports of men very 344
nobly held, can serve the world for no honest
use: therefore you must die. Come, headsman,
off with his head.

Par. O Lord, sir, let me live, or let me see my 348
death!

Inter. That shall you, and take your
leave of all your friends.   [*Unmuffling him.*]
So, look about you: know you any here?   352

Ber. Good morrow, noble captain.

2. Lord. God bless you, Captain Parolles.

1. Lord. God save you, noble captain.

2. Lord. Captain, what greeting will you 356
to my Lord Lafeu? I am for France.

1. Lord. Good captain, will you give me a
copy of the sonnet you writ to Diana in behalf of
the Count Rousillon? an I were not a very 360
coward I'd compel it of you; but fare you well.

    Exeunt [*all except Parolles and Interpreter*].

Inter. You are undone, captain, all but
your scarf; that has a knot on 't yet.

Par. Who cannot be crushed with a plot?   364

337 supposition: *imagination*
357 I am for: *I am about to set out for*   360 very: *complete*

Inter. If you could find out a country
where but women were that had received so
much shame, you might begin an impudent
nation. Fare ye well, sir; I am for France 368
too: we shall speak of you there.   *Exit.*
Par. Yet am I thankful: if my heart were great
'Twould burst at this. Captain I'll be no more;
But I will eat and drink, and sleep as soft   372
As captain shall: simply the thing I am
Shall make me live. Who knows himself a braggart,
Let him fear this; for it will come to pass
That every braggart shall be found an ass.   376
Rust, sword! cool, blushes! and Parolles, live
Safest in shame! being fool'd, by foolery thrive!
There's place and means for every man alive.
I'll after them.   *Exit.* 380

Scene Four

[Florence. A Room in the Widow's House]

Enter Helen, Widow, and Diana.

Hel. That you may well perceive I have not wrong'd
    you,
One of the greatest in the Christian world
Shall be my surety; 'fore whose throne 'tis needful,
Ere I can perfect mine intents, to kneel.   4
Time was I did him a desired office,
Dear almost as his life; which gratitude
Through flinty Tartar's bosom would peep forth,
And answer, thanks. I duly am inform'd   8
His Grace is at Marseilles; to which place
We have convenient convoy. You must know,

4 perfect mine intents: *carry out my purposes*   9 Marseilles; *cf. n.*

I am supposed dead: the army breaking,
My husband hies him home; where, heaven aiding,   12
And by the leave of my good lord the king,
We'll be before our welcome.
    Wid.   Gentle madam,
You never had a servant to whose trust
Your business was more welcome.
    Hel.   Nor you, mistress, 16
Ever a friend whose thoughts more truly labour
To recompense your love.   Doubt not but heaven
Hath brought me up to be your daughter's dower,
As it hath fated her to be my motive   20
And helper to a husband.   But, O strange men!
That can such sweet use make of what they hate,
When saucy trusting of the cozen'd thoughts
Defiles the pitchy night: so lust doth play   24
With what it loathes for that which is away.
But more of this hereafter.   You, Diana,
Under my poor instructions yet must suffer
Something in my behalf.
    Dia.   Let death and honesty   28
Go with your impositions, I am yours,
Upon your will to suffer.
    Hel.   Yet, I pray you:
But with the word the time will bring on summer,
When briers shall have leaves as well as thorns, 32
And be as sweet as sharp.   We must away;
Our wagon is prepar'd, and time revives us:
All's well that ends well: still the fine's the crown;
Whate'er the course, the end is the renown.   36
                                    Exeunt.

11 breaking: *disbanding*
14 be . . . welcome: *arrive before we are expected*
20 motive: *promoter*   23 saucy: *wanton*
28, 29 Let . . . impositions; *cf. n.*
30 Upon: *in accordance with*   Yet: *for a while*
31 with the word: *almost as I speak*   35 fine's: *end is*

Scene Five

[*Rousillon.   A Room in the Countess's Palace*]

Enter Clown, old Lady [*the Countess*], *and Lafeu.*

Laf. No, no, no; your son was misled with a
snipt-taffeta fellow there, whose villainous saffron
would have made all the unbaked and doughy
youth of a nation in his colour: your daughter-   4
in-law had been alive at this hour, and your son
here at home, more advanced by the king than
by that red-tailed humble-bee I speak of.

Count. I would I had not known him; it was   8
the death of the most virtuous gentlewoman
that ever nature had praise for creating.   If she
had partaken of my flesh, and cost me the dearest
groans of a mother, I could not have owed her 12
a more rooted love.

Laf. 'Twas a good lady, 'twas a good lady:
we may pick a thousand sallets ere we light on
such another herb.   16

Clo. Indeed, sir, she was the sweet-marjoram
of the sallet, or, rather the herb of grace.

Laf. They are not herbs, you knave;
they are nose-herbs.   20

Clo. I am no great Nebuchadnezzar, sir; I
have not much skill in grass.

Laf. Whether dost thou profess thyself, a
knave, or a fool?   24

Clo. A fool, sir, at a woman's service, and a
knave at a man's.

Laf. Your distinction?

2 snipt-taffeta: *dressed in slashed taffeta garments*   saffron: *yellow
dye (used in pastry)*   11 dearest: *most grievous*
15 sallets: *salads*   18 herb of grace: *rue*
19 herbs: *edible herbs*   20 nose-herbs: *scented flowers*

Clo. I would cozen the man of his wife, and 28
do his service.

Laf. So you were a knave at his service, indeed.

Clo. And I would give his wife my bauble, 32
sir, to do her service.

Laf. I will subscribe for thee, thou art both
knave and fool.

Clo. At your service.   36

Laf. No, no, no.

Clo. Why, sir, if I cannot serve you, I can
serve as great a prince as you are.

Laf. Who's that? a Frenchman?   40

Clo. Faith, sir, a' has an English name; but
his fisnomy is more hotter in France than
there.

Laf. What prince is that?   44

Clo. The black prince, sir; *alias,* the prince
of darkness; *alias,* the devil.

Laf. Hold thee, there's my purse. I give thee
not this to suggest thee from thy master thou 48
talkest of: serve him still.

Clo. I am a woodland fellow, sir, that always
loved a great fire; and the master I speak of
ever keeps a good fire. But, sure, he is the 52
prince of the world; let his nobility remain in's
court. I am for the house with the narrow gate,
which I take to be too little for pomp to enter:
some that humble themselves may; but the 56
many will be too chill and tender, and they'll
be for the flowery way that leads to the broad
gate and the great fire.

Laf. Go thy ways, I begin to be aweary of 60

42 fisnomy: *physiognomy*   48 suggest: *entice*

thee; and I tell thee so before, because I would
not fall out with thee. Go thy ways: let my
horses be well looked to, without any tricks.

Clo. If I put any tricks upon 'em, sir, they 64
shall be jade's tricks, which are their own right
by the law of nature.   *Exit.*

Laf. A shrewd knave and an unhappy.

Count. So a' is. My lord that's gone made 68
himself much sport out of him: by his authority
he remains here, which he thinks is a patent for
his sauciness; and, indeed, he has no pace, but
runs where he will.   72

Laf. I like him well; 'tis not amiss. And I
was about to tell you, since I heard of the good
lady's death, and that my lord your son was
upon his return home, I moved the king my 76
master to speak in the behalf of my daughter;
which, in the minority of them both, his majesty,
out of a self-gracious remembrance, did first
propose. His highness hath promised me to do 80
it; and to stop up the displeasure he hath con-
ceived against your son, there is no fitter matter.
How does your ladyship like it?

Count. With very much content, my lord, 84
and I wish it happily effected.

Laf. His highness comes post from Marseilles,
of as able body as when he numbered thirty: a'
will be here to-morrow, or I am deceived by him 88
that in such intelligence hath seldom failed.

Count. It rejoices me that I hope I shall see
him ere I die. I have letters that my son will be

65 jade's tricks; *cf. n.*
67 shrewd: *sharp of speech*   unhappy: *mischievous*
70 patent: *license*   71 pace: *training*
79 out . . . remembrance: *graciously and of his own motion*
87 numbered thirty: *was thirty years old*

here to-night: I shall beseech your lordship to 92
remain with me till they meet together.

Laf. Madam, I was thinking with what manners I might safely be admitted.

Count. You need but plead your honourable 96
privilege.

Laf. Lady, of that I have made a bold charter;
but I thank my God it holds yet.

[Re-]enter Clown.

Clo. O madam! yonder's my lord your son 100
with a patch of velvet on's face: whether there
be a scar under it or no, the velvet knows; but
'tis a goodly patch of velvet. His left cheek is a
cheek of two pile and a half, but his right cheek 104
is worn bare.

Laf. A scar nobly got, or a noble scar, is a
good livery of honour; so belike is that.

Clo. But it is your carbonadoed face.   108

Laf. Let us go see your son, I pray you: I
long to talk with the young noble soldier.

Clo. Faith, there's a dozen of 'em, with deli-
cate fine hats and most courteous feathers, which 112
bow the head and nod at every man.   *Exeunt.*

94, 95 with . . . admitted: *how I might becomingly gain admittance*
98 made . . . charter: *made daring use*   104 two . . . half; *cf. n.*
107 livery: *badge*   108 carbonadoed: *scored across, slashed*

ACT FIFTH

Scene One

[Marseilles.　A Street]

Enter Helen, Widow, and Diana, with two Attendants.

Hel. But this exceeding posting, day and night,
Must wear your spirits low; we cannot help it:
But since you have made the days and nights as one,
To wear your gentle limbs in my affairs,　　　　　　**4**
Be bold you do so grow in my requital
As nothing can unroot you.　In happy time!

Enter a gentle Astringer.

This man may help me to his majesty's ear,
If he would spend his power.　God save you, sir.　　**8**
　Gent. And you.
　Hel. Sir, I have seen you in the court of France.
　Gent. I have been sometimes there.
　Hel. I do presume, sir, that you are not fallen　　**12**
From the report that goes upon your goodness;
And therefore, goaded with most sharp occasions,
Which lay nice manners by, I put you to
The use of your own virtues, for the which　　　　**16**
I shall continue thankful.
　Gent.　　　　　　　　　What's your will?
　Hel. That it will please you
To give this poor petition to the king,
And aid me with that store of power you have　　　**20**

---

1 posting: *hastening*
5 bold: *sure*　　　　　grow . . . requital: *strengthen my intention to re-*
　　ward you　　　　　　　6 In . . . time: *this happens favorably*
S. d.　gentle Astringer: *gentleman-falconer*
8 spend: *use*　　　　　　　　13 goes upon: *is current concerning*
14 sharp occasions: *keen necessities*
15 lay . . . by: *put aside finical manners*　　put you to: *urge upon you*

To come into his presence.
　　Gent. The king's not here.
　　Hel.　　　　　　　　Not here, sir!
　　Gent.　　　　　　　　　　　　　Not, indeed:
He hence remov'd last night, and with more haste
Than is his use.
　　Wid.　　　　Lord, how we lose our pains!　　24
　　Hel. All's well that ends well yet,
Though time seem so adverse and means unfit.
I do beseech you, whither is he gone?
　　Gent. Marry, as I take it, to Rousillon,　　28
Whither I am going.
　　Hel.　　　　　　　I do beseech you, sir,
Since you are like to see the king before me,
Commend the paper to his gracious hand;
Which I presume shall render you no blame　　32
But rather make you thank your pains for it.
I will come after you with what good speed
Our means will make us means.
　　Gent.　　　　　　　　This I'll do for you.
　　Hel. And you shall find yourself to be well
　　　thank'd,　　　　　　　　　　　　　36
Whate'er falls more.　We must to horse again:
Go, go, provide.　　　　　　　　　　[*Exeunt.*]

Scene Two

[*Rousillon.　The inner Court of the
Countess's Palace*]

Enter Clown and Parolles.

　　Par. Good Monsieur Lavache, give my Lord
Lafeu this letter.　I have ere now, sir, been better

24 use: *custom*　　　37 Whate'er falls more: *whatever else occurs*

known to you, when I have held familiarity with
fresher clothes; but I am now, sir, muddied in 4
Fortune's mood, and smell somewhat strong of
her strong displeasure.

Clo. Truly, Fortune's displeasure is but slut-
tish if it smell so strongly as thou speakest of: I 8
will henceforth eat no fish of Fortune's butter-
ing. Prithee, allow the wind.

Par. Nay, you need not to stop your nose,
sir: I spake but by a metaphor.   12

Clo. Indeed, sir, if your metaphor stink, I
will stop my nose; or against any man's metaphor. Prithee, get thee further.

Par. Pray you, sir, deliver me this paper.   16

Clo. Foh! prithee, stand away: a paper from
Fortune's close-stool to give to a nobleman!
Look, here he comes himself.

Enter Lafeu.

Here is a purr of Fortune's, sir, or of Fortune's 20
cat—but not a musk-cat—that has fallen into
the unclean fishpond of her displeasure, and, as
he says, is muddied withal. Pray you, sir, use
the carp as you may, for he looks like a poor, 24
decayed, ingenious, foolish, rascally knave. I do
pity his distress in my similes of comfort, and
leave him to your lordship.   [*Exit.*]

Par. My lord, I am a man whom Fortune 28
hath cruelly scratched.

Laf. And what would you have me to do? 'tis
too late to pare her nails now. Wherein have
you played the knave with Fortune that she 32
should scratch you, who of herself is a good lady,

3 held familiarity: *been acquainted*   5 mood: *anger*
10 allow the wind: *let me get to windward of you*

and would not have knaves thrive long under
[her]? There's a cardecu for you. Let the justices
make you and Fortune friends; I am for other 36
business.

Par. I beseech your honour to hear me one
single word.

Laf. You beg a single penny more: come, 40
you shall ha 't; save your word.

Par. My name, my good lord, is Parolles.

Laf. You beg more than [one] word then.
Cox my passion! give me your hand. How 44
does your drum?

Par. O, my good lord! you were the first that
found me.

Laf. Was I, in sooth? and I was the first 48
that lost thee.

Par. It lies in you, my lord, to bring me in
some grace, for you did bring me out.

Laf. Out upon thee, knave! dost thou put 52
upon me at once both the office of God and the
devil? one brings thee in grace and the other
brings thee out. [*Trumpets sound.*] The king's
coming; I know by his trumpets. Sirrah, in- 56
quire further after me; I had talk of you last
night: though you are a fool and a knave, you
shall eat: go to, follow.

Par. I praise God for you.   [*Exeunt.*] 60

35, 36 Let . . . friends; *cf. n.*   44 Cox my passion; *God's passion*
50, 51 in some grace; *into some favor*

Scene Three

[The Same.   A Room in the Countess's Palace]

Flourish.   Enter King, old Lady [the Countess],
Lafeu, the two French Lords, with Attendants.

King. We lost a jewel of her, and our esteem
Was made much poorer by it: but your son,
As mad in folly, lack'd the sense to know
Her estimation home.

Count.   'Tis past, my liege;   **4**
And I beseech your majesty to make it
Natural rebellion, done i' the blaze of youth,
When oil and fire, too strong for reason's force,
O'erbears it and burns on.

King.   My honour'd lady,   **8**
I have forgiven and forgotten all,
Though my revenges were high bent upon him,
And watch'd the time to shoot.

Laf.   This I must say—
But first I beg my pardon—the young lord   **12**
Did to his majesty, his mother, and his lady,
Offence of mighty note, but to himself
The greatest wrong of all: he lost a wife
Whose beauty did astonish the survey   **16**
Of richest eyes, whose words all ears took captive,
Whose dear perfection hearts that scorn'd to serve
Humbly call'd mistress.

King.   Praising what is lost
Makes the remembrance dear.   Well, call him hither; **20**
We are reconcil'd, and the first view shall kill
All repetition.   Let him not ask our pardon:

---

1 our esteem: *the value of our kingdom*   3 As: *as if*
4 estimation: *worth*   home: *thoroughly*   5 make: *consider*
10 high bent upon: *strongly directed against*
17 richest: *most experienced*   22 repetition: *reference to what is past*

The nature of his great offence is dead,
And deeper than oblivion we do bury   24
Th' incensing relics of it.   Let him approach,
A stranger, no offender; and inform him
So 'tis our will he should.
 Gent.   I shall, my liege.
              [Exit.]
 King. What says he to your daughter? have you
   spoke?   28
 Laf. All that he is hath reference to your highness.
 King. Then shall we have a match.   I have letters
   sent me,
That sets him high in fame.

     Enter Count Bertram.

 Laf.   He looks well on 't.
 King. I am not a day of season,   32
For thou mayst see a sunshine and a hail
In me at once; but to the brightest beams
Distracted clouds give way: so stand thou forth;
The time is fair again.
 Ber.   My high-repented blames, 36
Dear sovereign, pardon to me.
 King.   All is whole;
Not one word more of the consumed time.
Let's take the instant by the forward top,
For we are old, and on our quick'st decrees   40
Th' inaudible and noiseless foot of time
Steals ere we can effect them.   You remember
The daughter of this lord?
 Ber. Admiringly, my liege: 44

29 hath reference to: *is dependent upon*
31 He . . . on 't: *his appearance bears it out*
32 of season: *seasonable*
36 high-repented blames: *deeply repented faults*
38 consumed: *past*
39 instant: *present moment*   forward top: *forelock*

At first I stuck my choice upon her, ere my heart
Durst make too bold a herald of my tongue,
Where the impression of mine eye enfixing,
Contempt his scornful perspective did lend me,   48
Which warp'd the line of every other favour;
Scorn'd a fair colour, or express'd it stolen;
Extended or contracted all proportions
To a most hideous object.   Thence it came   52
That she, whom all men prais'd, and whom myself,
Since I have lost, have lov'd, was in mine eye
The dust that did offend it.
    King.   Well excus'd:
That thou didst love her, strikes some scores away   56
From the great compt.   But love that comes too late,
Like a remorseful pardon slowly carried,
To the great sender turns a sour offence,
Crying, 'That's good that's gone.'   Our rash faults   60
Make trivial price of serious things we have,
Not knowing them until we know their grave:
Oft our displeasures, to ourselves unjust,
Destroy our friends and after weep their dust: 64
Our own love waking cries to see what's done,
While shameful hate sleeps out the afternoon.
Be this sweet Helen's knell, and now forget her.
Send forth your amorous token for fair Maudlin: 68
The main consents are had; and here we'll stay
To see our widower's second marriage-day,
Which better than the first, O dear heaven, bless!
Or, ere they meet, in me, O nature, cesse!   72
    Laf. Come on, my son, in whom my house's name
Must be digested, give a favour from you
To sparkle in the spirits of my daughter,

---

48 perspective: *instrument for producing optical illusions*
50 express'd: *declared*   57 compt: *account*
66 *Cf. n.*   72 cesse: *cease*   74 digested: *amalgamated*

That she may quickly come.

                        [Bertram gives a ring.]
                      By my old beard,   **76**
And every hair that's on 't, Helen, that's dead,
Was a sweet creature; such a ring as this,
The last that e'er I took her leave at court,
I saw upon her finger.

   Ber.   Hers it was not.   **80**

   King. Now, pray you, let me see it; for mine eye,
While I was speaking, oft was fasten'd to 't.—
This ring was mine; and, when I gave it Helen,
I bade her, if her fortunes ever stood   **84**
Necessitied to help, that by this token
I would relieve her. Had you that craft to reave her
Of what should stead her most?

   Ber.   My gracious sovereign,
Howe'er it pleases you to take it so,   **88**
The ring was never hers.

   Count.   Son, on my life,
I have seen her wear it; and she reckon'd it
At her life's rate.

   Laf.   I am sure I saw her wear it.

   Ber. You are deceiv'd, my lord, she never saw it: **92**
In Florence was it from a casement thrown me,
Wrapp'd in a paper, which contain'd the name
Of her that threw it. Noble she was, and thought
I stood ingag'd: but when I had subscrib'd   **96**
To mine own fortune, and inform'd her fully
I could not answer in that course of honour
As she had made the overture, she ceas'd
In heavy satisfaction, and would never   **100**

79 The last: *the last time*   85 Necessitied to help: *in need of help*
96 ingag'd: *unengaged*
96, 97 subscrib'd . . . fortune: *admitted the state of my fortunes*
98, 99 I . . . overture: *I could not pursue the honorable course she
   suggested*   100 heavy satisfaction: *sorrowful acquiescence*

Receive the ring again.

    King.   Plutus himself,
That knows the tinct and multiplying medicine,
Hath not in nature's mystery more science
Than I have in this ring: 'twas mine, 'twas Helen's, 104
Whoever gave it you.   Then, if you know
That you are well acquainted with yourself,
Confess 'twas hers, and by what rough enforcement
You got it from her. She call'd the saints to surety, 108
That she would never put it from her finger,
Unless she gave it to yourself in bed,
Where you have never come, or sent it us
Upon her great disaster.

    Ber.   She never saw it.   112

    King. Thou speak'st it falsely, as I love **mine**
      honour,
And mak'st conjectural fears to come into me
Which I would fain shut out. If it should prove
That thou art so inhuman—'twill not prove so—   116
And yet I know not: thou didst hate her deadly,
And she is dead; which nothing, but to close
Her eyes myself, could win me to believe,
More than to see this ring.   Take him away.   120
                       [*Guards seize Bertram.*]
My fore-past proofs, howe'er the matter fall,
Shall tax my fears of little vanity,
Having vainly fear'd too little.   Away with him!
We'll sift this matter further.

    Ber.   If you shall prove 124
This ring was ever hers, you shall as easy
Prove that I husbanded her bed in Florence,
Where yet she never was.   [*Exit guarded.*]

102 tinct: *tincture*   multiplying medicine: *chemical which multi-*
    plies gold   103 science: *knowledge*
105, 106 if . . . yourself: *if you know what is best for yourself*
112 Upon: *at the time of*   121-123 My . . . little; *cf. n.*

King. I am wrapp'd in dismal thinkings.

    Enter a Gentleman [the Astringer].

Gent.   Gracious sovereign, 128
Whether I have been to blame or no, I know not:
Here's a petition from a Florentine,
Who hath for four or five removes come short
To tender it herself. I undertook it,   132
Vanquish'd thereto by the fair grace and speech
Of the poor suppliant, who by this I know
Is here attending: her business looks in her
With an importing visage, and she told me,   136
In a sweet verbal brief, it did concern
Your highness with herself.

    [King reads] a Letter. 'Upon his many pro-
testations to marry me when his wife was dead, I 140
blush to say it, he won me. Now is the Count Rousillon a widower: his vows are forfeited to me,
and my honour's paid to him. He stole from
Florence, taking no leave, and I follow him to 144
his country for justice. Grant it me, O king! in
you it best lies; otherwise a seducer flourishes,
and a poor maid is undone.

                        Diana Capilet.' 148

Laf. I will buy me a son-in-law in a fair, and
toll for this: I'll none of him.

King. The heavens have thought well on thee, Lafeu,
To bring forth this discovery. Seek these suitors. 152
Go speedily and bring again the count.

                [Exeunt some Attendants.]

131 removes: *days' journeys*
131, 132 come . . . tender: *fallen short of tendering*
135, 136 looks . . . visage: *seems, from her appearance, to be important*
138 with: *as well as*
145, 146 in . . . lies: *it is most in your power*
150 toll for: *take out a license to sell*

Enter Bertram [guarded].

I am afeard the life of Helen, lady,
Was foully snatch'd.
   Count.   Now, justice on the doers!
   King. I wonder, sir, sith wives are monsters to
    you,   156
And that you fly them as you swear them lordship,
Yet you desire to marry.

*Enter Widow, Diana, and Parolles [with
Attendants].*

                               What woman's that?
   Dia. I am, my lord, a wretched Florentine,
Derived from the ancient Capilet: 160
My suit, as I do understand, you know,
And therefore know how far I may be pitied.
   Wid. I am her mother, sir, whose age and honour
Both suffer under this complaint we bring,   164
And both shall cease, without your remedy.
   King. Come hither, count; do you know these
    women?
   Ber. My lord, I neither can nor will deny
But that I know them: do they charge me further? 168
   Dia. Why do you look so strange upon your wife?
   Ber. She's none of mine, my lord.
   Dia.   If you shall marry,
You give away this hand, and that is mine;
You give away heaven's vows, and those are mine; 172
You give away myself, which is known mine;
For I by vow am so embodied yours
That she which marries you must marry me:
Either both or none.   176
    Laf. [*To Bertram.*] Your reputation comes

156 sith: *since*   160 Derived: *descended*   165 cease: *die*

too short for my daughter: you are no husband
for her.

Ber. My lord, this is a fond and desperate crea-
ture,   180
Whom sometime I have laugh'd with: let your highness
Lay a more noble thought upon mine honour
Than for to think that I would sink it here.

King. Sir, for my thoughts, you have them ill to
friend,   184
Till your deeds gain them: fairer prove your honour,
Than in my thought it lies.

Dia.   Good my lord,
Ask him upon his oath, if he does think
He had not my virginity.   188

King. What sayst thou to her?

Ber.   She's impudent, my lord;
And was a common gamester to the camp.

Dia. He does me wrong, my lord; if I were so,
He might have bought me at a common price: 192
Do not believe him.   O! behold this ring,
Whose high respect and rich validity
Did lack a parallel; yet for all that
He gave it to a commoner o' the camp,   196
If I be one.

Count.   He blushes, and 'tis hit:
Of six preceding ancestors, that gem
Conferr'd by testament to the sequent issue,
Hath it been ow'd and worn.   This is his wife: 200
That ring's a thousand proofs.

King.   Methought you said
You saw one here in court could witness it.

Dia. I did, my lord, but loath am to produce

184 you . . . friend: *they are unfriendly to you*
190 gamester: *harlot*   194 respect: *esteem*   validity: *value*
197 'tis hit: *it is discovered*

So bad an instrument: his name's Parolles.   204
                          [*Exit Parolles covertly.*]
   Laf. I saw the man to-day, if man he be.
   King. Find him, and bring him hither.
                                    [*Exit an Attendant.*]
   Ber.   What of him?
He's quoted for a most perfidious slave,
With all the spots of the world tax'd and debosh'd, 208
Whose nature sickens but to speak a truth.
Am I or that or this for what he'll utter,
That will speak anything?
   King.   She hath that ring of yours.
   Ber. I think she has: certain it is I lik'd her,   212
And boarded her i' the wanton way of youth.
She knew her distance and did angle for me,
Madding my eagerness with her restraint,
As all impediments in fancy's course   216
Are motives of more fancy; and, in fine,
Her infinite cunning, with her modern grace,
Subdued me to her rate: she got the ring,
And I had that which any inferior might   220
At market-price have bought.
   Dia.   I must be patient;
You, that have turn'd off a first so noble wife,
May justly diet me.   I pray you yet—
Since you lack virtue I will lose a husband—   224
Send for your ring; I will return it home,
And give me mine again.
   Ber.   I have it not.
   King. What ring was yours, I pray you?
   Dia.   Sir, much like

204 instrument: *agent*   207 quoted: *cited*
210 *Am I to be judged according to what he will say?*
215 Madding: *maddening*   218 modern: *commonplace*
219 Subdued . . . rate: *forced me to agree to her price*
223 diet me: *deprive me of my due*

The same upon your finger.   228

   King. Know you this ring? this ring was his of late.

   Dia. And this was it I gave him, being a-bed.

   King. The story then goes false you threw it him
Out of a casement.

   Dia.   I have spoke the truth.   232

      [Re-]enter Parolles [with Attendant.]

   Ber. My lord, I do confess the ring was hers.

   King. You boggle shrewdly, every feather starts you.
Is this the man you speak of?

   Dia.   Ay, my lord.

   King. Tell me, sirrah, but tell me true, I charge
     you,   236
Not fearing the displeasure of your master—
Which on your just proceeding I'll keep off—
By him and by this woman here what know you?

   Par. So please your majesty, my master hath 240
been an honourable gentleman.   Tricks he hath
had in him, which gentlemen have.

   King. Come, come, to the purpose: did he
love this woman?   244

   Par. Faith, sir, he did love her; but how?

   King. How, I pray you?

   Par. He did love her, sir, as a gentleman
loves a woman.   248

   King. How is that?

   Par. He loved her, sir, and loved her not.

   King. As thou art a knave, and no knave,—
what an equivocal companion is this!   252

   Par. I am a poor man, and at your majesty's
command.

234 boggle shrewdly: *change about vilely*   starts: *startles*
238 on . . . proceeding: *if you act honorably*
239 By: *concerning*

Laf. He's a good drum, my lord, but a
naughty orator.   256

Dia. Do you know he promised me marriage?

Par. Faith, I know more than I'll speak.

King. But wilt thou not speak all thou
knowest?   260

Par. Yes, so please your majesty. I did go
between them, as I said; but more than that, he
loved her, for, indeed, he was mad for her, and
talked of Satan, and of limbo, and of Furies, 264
and I know not what: yet I was in that credit
with them at that time, that I knew of their
going to bed, and of other motions, as promising
her marriage, and things which would derive 268
me ill will to speak of: therefore I will not
speak what I know.

King. Thou hast spoken all already, unless
thou canst say they are married: but thou art 272
too fine in thy evidence; therefore stand aside.
This ring, you say, was yours?

Dia. Ay, my good lord.

King. Where did you buy it? or who gave it you? 276

Dia. It was not given me, nor I did not buy it.

King. Who lent it you?

Dia.   It was not lent me neither.

King. Where did you find it, then?

Dia.   I found it not.

King. If it were yours by none of all these ways, 280
How could you give it him?

Dia.   I never gave it him.

Laf. This woman's an easy glove, my lord:
she goes off and on at pleasure.

King. This ring was mine: I gave it his first wife. 284

255 drum: *drummer*   256 naughty: *worthless*
267 motions: *acts*   273 fine: *finical*

Dia. It might be yours or hers, for aught I know.

King. Take her away; I do not like her now.

To prison with her; and away with him.

Unless thou tell'st me where thou hadst this ring   288

Thou diest within this hour.

Dia.   I'll never tell you.

King. Take her away.

Dia.   I'll put in bail, my liege.

King. I think thee now some common customer.

Dia. By Jove, if ever I knew man, 'twas you.   292

King. Wherefore hast thou accus'd him all this
   while?

Dia. Because he's guilty, and he is not guilty.

He knows I am no maid, and he'll swear to 't;

I'll swear I am a maid, and he knows not.   296

Great king, I am no strumpet, by my life;

I am either maid, or else this old man's wife.

                    [*Pointing to Lafeu.*]

King. She does abuse our ears: to prison with her!

Dia. Good mother, fetch my bail. [*Exit Widow.*]

   Stay, royal sir;   300

The jeweller that owes the ring is sent for,

And he shall surety me.   But for this lord,

Who hath abus'd me, as he knows himself,

Though yet he never harm'd me, here I quit him: 304

He knows himself my bed he hath defil'd,

And at that time he got his wife with child:

Dead though she be, she feels her young one kick:

So there's my riddle: one that's dead is quick;   308

And now behold the meaning.

                    Enter Helen and Widow.

   King.   Is there no exorcist

291 customer: *harlot*   304 quit: *acquit*
308 quick: *alive, with child (used punningly)*
309 exorcist: *raiser of dead spirits*

Beguiles the truer office of mine eyes?
Is 't real that I see?

    Hel.   No, my good lord;
'Tis but the shadow of a wife you see;   312
The name and not the thing.

    Ber.   Both, both. O pardon!

    Hel. O my good lord! when I was like this maid,
I found you wondrous kind. There is your ring;
And, look you, here's your letter; this it says: 316
'When from my finger you can get this ring,
And are by me with child, &c.' This is done:
Will you be mine, now you are doubly won?

    Ber. If she, my liege, can make me know this
        clearly,   320
I'll love her dearly, ever, ever dearly.

    Hel. If it appear not plain, and prove untrue,
Deadly divorce step between me and you!
O! my dear mother, do I see you living?   324

    Laf. Mine eyes smell onions; I shall weep
anon. [*To Parolles.*] Good Tom Drum, lend
me a handkercher: so, I thank thee. Wait on
me home, I'll make sport with thee: let thy 328
curtsies alone, they are scurvy ones.

    King. Let us from point to point this story know,
To make the even truth in pleasure flow.
[*To Diana.*] If thou be'st yet a fresh uncropped
        flower,   332
Choose thou thy husband, and I'll pay thy dower;
For I can guess that by thy honest aid
Thou kept'st a wife herself, thyself a maid.
Of that, and all the progress, more and less,   336
Resolvedly more leisure shall express:

331 even: *straightforward*   336 progress: *course of the affair*
337 Resolvedly: *until all is explained*

All yet seems well; and if it end so meet,
The bitter past, more welcome is the sweet.

Flourish.

[EPILOGUE.

Spoken by the King.]

The king's a beggar, now the play is done:
All is well ended if this suit be won
That you express content; which we will pay,
With strife to please you, day exceeding day: 4
Ours be your patience then, and yours our parts;
Your gentle hands lend us, and take our hearts.

Exeunt omnes.

338 meet: *fittingly*   6 hands: *applause*

FINIS.

NOTES

I. i. 63, 64. *I do affect a sorrow indeed, but I have it too.* Helena means that she affects a grief for her father, but feels a real grief at the departure of Bertram. Her other cryptic utterances in this scene hint at her love for Bertram, which she conceals behind a veil of obscure and ambiguous speech.

I. i. 67, 68. *If the living be enemy to the grief, the excess makes it soon mortal.* 'If Bertram returned your love, your joy would overbalance your grief.'

I. i. 70. *How understand we that?* Lafeu's question refers to the Countess' remark: he has just perceived that it contained some hidden meaning. Perhaps, as Coleridge suggests, Lafeu and Bertram speak at once.

I. i. 82, 83. *He cannot want the best That shall attend his love.* The sense is obscure. Perhaps it is that Bertram can never lack the best service of those who, like Lafeu, follow him because they love him.

I. i. 85, 86. *The best wishes that can be forged in your thoughts be servants to you!* 'May your dearest wishes be fulfilled.'

I. i. 92, 93. *And these great tears grace his remembrance more Than those I shed for him.* The tears she now sheds for Bertram are, to those who mistake their cause, a greater tribute to her father than those she shed at his death.

I. i. 100, 101. *In his bright radiance and collateral light Must I be comforted, not in his sphere.* An allusion to the Ptolemaic system of astronomy, according to which there were eight concentric spheres surrounding the earth. Each star or planet was limited to one of these spheres, but its light penetrated the others.

I. i. 116. *Looks.* The third person plural present

indicative of Shakespearean verbs not infrequently end in s: cf. II. iii. 127, III. iv. 15, III. v. 25.

I. i. 120, 121. *No. And no.* Parolles disclaims any right to the title of monarch, and Helena in turn repudiates the name of queen.

I. i. 154, 155. *should be buried in highways, out of all sanctified limit.* It was forbidden to bury suicides in consecrated ground: they were frequently interred at a crossroads.

I. i. 158. *his.* The regular possessive case of 'it' in Shakespeare. 'Its' occurs but seldom.

I. i. 182-191. Helena catalogues the endearing nicknames by which Bertram will address his (supposititious) sweethearts at the French court. Under the stress of dissembling her emotion she speaks somewhat incoherently.

I. i. 214, 215. *predominant, retrograde.* Astrological terms. A planet is generally benign in its influence when it is predominant, and malignant when it is retrograde.

I. i. 222. *a virtue of a good wing.* A reference to the popular sport of falconry. The insinuation is that Parolles is apt in flight, which would be a virtue in a hawk, but which is a reproach to a soldier.

I. i. 231-233. *When thou hast leisure, say thy prayers; when thou hast none, remember thy friends.* Parolles is already affecting the cynical philosophy which he believes suitable to a courtier. The advice may be paraphrased, 'Say your prayers when you can find nothing better to do, and remember your friends only when you are too busy to serve them.'

I. i. 241, 242. *The mightiest space in fortune nature brings To join like likes, and kiss like native things.* 'Across the gulf of the greatest disparity in fortune, nature brings kindred spirits to join each other, and to kiss like people born to each other's society.'

I. ii. *1. Lord.* The 1. Lord and 2. Lord of this
scene are, in the Folio, called '1 Lo. G.' and '2 Lo. E.'
The initials, as Capell suggested, are probably those
of the actors who played these parts. These initials
are used in all the other scenes (II. i, III. i, ii, vi, IV.
i, iii) in which the two French lords appear, although
the title preceding the initial is sometimes 'Lord,'
sometimes 'French' and sometimes 'Cap[tain].' At
the beginning of IV. i the 1. Lord is described by the
Folio as '1 Lord E.,' and the error in the initial persists
throughout the scene. It is clear from the dialogue in
III. vi and IV. iii that it is '1 Lord G.' who undertakes
and carries out the capture of Parolles.

I. ii. 33-35. *but they may jest Till their own scorn
return to them unnoted Ere they can hide their levity
in honour.* 'Your father had the same airy flights of
satirical wit with the young lords of the present time,
but they do not what he did, hide their unnoted levity
in honour, cover petty faults with great merit.' (John-
son.)

I. ii. 36-38. *So like a courtier, contempt nor bitterness Were in his pride or sharpness; if they were, His
equal had awak'd them.* 'As was fitting in a courtier,
he exhibited neither contempt in his pride, nor bitterness in his sharp strokes of wit, except when he was
provoked by an equal.'

I. ii. 44, 45. *Making them proud of his humility In
their poor praise he humbled.* 'Making them proud
by his humble acceptance of their praises, which he
rendered inadequate by the nobility of his actions.'

I. ii. 50, 51. *So in approof lives not his epitaph As
in your royal speech.* 'His virtues are testified to no-
where so eloquently as in your royal speech.'

I. iii. 57, 58. *young Charbon the puritan, and old
Poysam the papist.* The two names are probably cor-
ruptions of 'Chairbonne' and 'Poisson,' referring to
the lenten diets of the two sects.

I. iii. 60. *joul horns together.* The standing Elizabethan jest alluding to the horns that were supposed
to grow upon the forehead of a wronged husband.

I. iii. 68. *cuckoo.* Another stock pleasantry on
the same subject, playing on the words 'cuckoo' and
'cuckold.' Cf. *Love's Labour's Lost*, V. ii. 902-910.

I. iii. 98-101. The puritan clergy thought the surplice savoured too much of Roman Catholicism: they
preferred to wear a simple black gown. However, as
the laws of the church required the use of the surplice, they wore it, but *over* the gown.

I. iii. 159, 160. *That this distemper'd messenger of
wet, The many-colour'd Iris, rounds thine eye.* Henley
explains this as a reference to 'that suffusion of
colours which glimmers around the sight when the
eyelashes are wet with tears.'

II. i. 12-14. *let higher Italy—Those bated that inherit but the fall Of the last monarchy—.* A much-
disputed passage. The meaning may be, 'Let the
Italian nobles, except those whose rank is the gift of
the last revolution (and whose opinions on matters of
honour are therefore of no account).'

II. i. 33. *But one to dance with!* Ceremonial
swords were a part of court dress.

II. i. 36, 37. *our parting is a tortured body.*
'Parting us is as painful as dismembering a body.'

II. i. 87, 88. *more Than I dare blame my weakness.*
'To such a degree that I cannot attribute it entirely
to credulity on my part.'

II. i. 114, 115. *wherein the honour Of my dear
father's gift stands chief in power.* 'In the cure of
which my father's gift is reputed most powerful.

II. i. 167. *her.* This is the reading of the Folio,
and there is nothing to show that Shakespeare is not
responsible for this mistake in the sex of Hesperus.

II. i. 176. *nay worse—if worse—extended.* This
is the most satisfactory emendation of the obviously

corrupt reading of the Folio: 'ne worse of worst extended.'

II. ii. 25. *as Tib's rush for Tom's forefinger.* Rush rings were frequently exchanged by country lovers who decided to dispense with the marriage ceremony.

II. iii. 34. *facinerious.* Parolles' error for 'facinorous' (='infamous').

II. iii. 50. *Mort du vinaigre.* Literally, 'By the death of the vinegar,' i.e. 'By the Crucifixion.'

II. iii. 64. *to each but one.* This may mean either 'but one wife to each of you' or 'to each of you, with one exception (i.e. Bertram).'

II. iii. 84, 85. *I had rather be in this choice than throw ames-ace for my life.* 'Ames-ace'=two aces, the lowest throw at dice. Lafeu ironically contrasts such ill luck with the good luck of being in this choice.

II. iii. 159. *misprision.* A play on two meanings of the word: 'wrongful imprisonment' and 'lack of appreciation.'

II. iii. 234. *Well, I shall be wiser—.* Presumably Parolles intends to conclude with some such words as 'than to attack an old man,' but Lafeu purposely misunderstands him.

II. iii. 246. *as I will by thee.* Lafeu plays on the word 'past': the meaning is 'I will pass by thee.'

II. iii. 314. *these balls bound; there's noise in it.* 'The noise which these balls make when they bounce shows that they are good': i.e. 'Your words show that you have proper spirit.'

II. v. 41, 42. *like him that leaped into the custard.* It was a favorite amusement at city entertainments for a jester to leap into a large custard.

III. i. 12, 13. *That the great figure of a council frames By self-unable motion.* 'Who forms his ideas of a great council by the sole aid of his own insufficient mental powers.'

III. ii. 92, 93. *The fellow has a deal of that too*

much, Which holds him much to have. 'The fellow has too much of that quality (persuasiveness) which stands him in such good stead.'

III. iv. 4. *Saint Jaques' pilgrim.* The shrine has not been identified.

III. iv. 13. *his despiteful Juno.* A reference to the labors of Hercules, imposed upon him by Juno.

III. v. S. d. *Violenta.* No speech is assigned to Violenta by the Folio. It is possible that she was a speaking character in an earlier version of the play, and that her lines were cancelled in a subsequent revision, while the presence of her name in this stage-direction was overlooked.

III. vi. 40. *John Drum's entertainment.* Giving a man a beating, or throwing him out of doors, was sometimes called John (or Tom) Drum's entertainment.

III. vi. 65. *hic jacet.* 'Here lies—': the common beginning of epitaphs. Parolles means that he would get the drum or die in the attempt.

III. vii. 3. *But I shall lose the grounds I work upon.* 'Unless I give up the only advantage I possess.' The only further proof of her identity which Helena can offer is the evidence of Bertram, and to disclose herself to him would be to defeat her purpose.

IV. i. 46. *Bajazet's mule.* Probably Parolles' error for 'Balaam's ass.' He wishes to exchange a prattling tongue for one which speaks but seldom, and then only by inspiration.

IV. ii. 25. *Jove's.* Quite possibly Shakespeare wrote 'God's,' which was altered to the present word in deference to the laws against blasphemy on the stage. The general meaning of the passage would then be, 'Who would believe me, if I swore by God that I would break His laws?'

IV. ii. 30. *unseal'd.* A bond without a seal is invalid.

IV. ii. 38. *I see that men make rope's in such a scarre.* This line is hopelessly corrupt.

IV. iii. 31, 32. *Is it not meant damnable in us, to be trumpeters of our unlawful intents?* 'Do we not court damnation in parading our unlawful intentions?' Most editors emend 'most' for 'meant.'

IV. iii. 255. *Half won is match well made; match, and well make it.* 'A bargain in which you receive half your price in advance is a good one; adopt this course.'

IV. iii. 283. *Nessus.* The centaur who attempted to carry off Deïaneira.

IV. iii. 314-317. The legal phrases in this speech are all taken from the form for the absolute conveyance of real property.

IV. iv. 9. *Marseilles.* This should be pronounced as a tri-syllabic word. The spellings of the Folio are *Marcellae* and *Marcellus.*

IV. iv. 28, 29. *Let death and honesty Go with your impositions.* 'Even unto death, if your commands are honest.'

IV. v. 65. *jade's tricks.* Used punningly: a jade is a horse, a jade's trick is a sharp practice.

IV. v. 104. *two pile and a half.* The quality of velvet is determined by the height of the pile or nap, under the terms 'double-pile,' 'triple-pile,' etc.

V. ii. 35, 36. *Let the justices make you and Fortune friends.* 'Let the justices of the peace award you a maintenance out of the funds for the poor.'

V. iii. 66. *While shameful hate sleeps out the afternoon.* 'While shameful hate, having done its worst, is indifferent to the distress it has caused.'

V. iii. 121-123. *My fore-past proofs, howe'er the matter fall, Shall tax my fears of little vanity, Having vainly fear'd too little.* 'No matter what my conclusions may be, I shall not be ashamed of having feared too much, since it is clear from what I have heard that until now I have been too unsuspecting.'

APPENDIX A

Sources of the Play

The source of the main plot of *All's Well that Ends Well* is the ninth novel of the third day of Boccaccio's *Decameron,* as translated by William Painter in *The Palace of Pleasure* (1566). Painter's synopsis of the story is as follows:

'Giletta a phisician's doughter of Narbon, healed the Frenche Kyng of a fistula, for reward whereof she demaunded Beltramo Counte of Rossiglione to husbande. The Counte beyng maried againste his will, for despite fled to Florence and loved an other. Giletta his wife, by pollicie founde meanes to lye with her husbande, in place of his lover, and was begotten with child of two soonnes: which knowen to her husbande, he received her againe, and afterwardes he lived in greate honor and felicitie.'

The most significant features of Boccaccio's story which Shakespeare altered are these: Giletta is rich; she is not the foster-sister of Bertram, though brought up with him; and the King of France is not present to act as *deus ex machina* in the final reconciliation. Boccaccio's tale is related chiefly for the sake of the plot, and so far as the character-portraits of Helena, Bertram and the King are concerned Shakespeare's debt to his original is negligible. There are no counterparts in the novel for the Countess, Lafeu, Lavache or any of the persons of the sub-plot which recounts the adventures and downfall of Parolles. For this sub-plot and for the character of Parolles no sources have been found, although various books have been suggested from which Shakespeare might have drawn a few minor incidents or expressions.

APPENDIX B

THE HISTORY OF THE PLAY

The early history of *All's Well that Ends Well* has long been the subject of controversy. In 1598 Francis Meres, in his *Palladis Tamia,* referred to Shakespeare as the author of a play called *Love's Labour's Won.* It has been almost universally assumed that this play has not been lost, but that it was re-named before publication. Five or six of Shakespeare's comedies have been identified with *Love's Labour's Won* by various editors, but the theory of Dr. Farmer, put forth in 1767, that the play is the one known to us as *All's Well that Ends Well,* has been concurred in by the majority of critics. The internal evidence, on which alone this theory rests, is fairly convincing. The older title certainly fits the plot of the play admirably. Moreover, two speeches in the fifth act seem to refer directly to that title, and in the second of these speeches there is also an unmistakable allusion to the present name of the play:

Will you be mine, now you are doubly won?

V. iii. 319

All is well ended if this suit be won. . . .

V. iii. 341

If Dr. Farmer's conjecture is correct, *All's Well* must have been written by 1598, but many critics place its composition much earlier than this, and a few place it as late as 1606. The evidence (which is again entirely internal) is extremely confusing. The frequent rhymed passages and the letters in verse are characteristic of Shakespeare's earlier work: on the other hand, there are many speeches (e.g. that of the King, I. ii. 24-48) in the involved elliptical style of the author's later period. Perhaps the most satis-

factory, and certainly the most commonly received,
solution of the problem is to assume that *All's Well*
as we have it is the revised form of an early play.
This view is strengthened by the existence of some
awkward breaks in the text (notably that at I. i. 181)
which may be due to the imperfect joining of the older
and the newer versions.

All's Well that Ends Well was first printed in the
Folio of 1623, and it did not achieve a separate publication until 1734.[1] There is no record of its having
been performed in Shakespeare's lifetime or, indeed,
for more than a century after his death. The play was
included in a seventeenth century 'Catalogue of part
of His Ma^tes Servants Playes as they were formerly
acted at the Blackfryers & now allowed of to his Ma^tes
Servants at ye New Theatre,'[2] but there is nothing to
show that Killigrew ever took advantage of this license. At length, on February 24, 1740-1, the
following advertisement appeared in *The London
Daily Post, and General Advertiser:* 'For the Benefit
of Mrs. Giffard. At the Late Theatre in *Goodman's-
Fields,* Saturday, March 7, will be performed A Con-
cert . . . N.B. Between the Two Parts of the Con-
cert, will be reviv'd a Play, call'd All's Well That
Ends Well. Written by Shakespear, and never performed since his Time. . . . the part of Helena by
Mrs. Giffard, with an Epilogue adapted to that Character. . . .'

This performance seems to have been sufficiently
successful to incite emulation. The play was put on
ten times at Drury Lane during the season of 1741-2
with T. Cibber as Parolles and Mrs. Woffington as
Helena. Covent Garden followed suit in 1746, when

---

[1] The 'edition' of 1714 noted by Lowndes is merely a copy
of the play removed from the eight-volume edition of Rowe.

[2] This catalogue is reproduced on pp. 316-317 of *A History of Restoration Drama* by Allardyce Nicoll, who gives
its date as c. Jan 12, 1668-9.

a performance for Cibber's benefit was arranged for April 1, but as Cibber returned to Drury Lane before that date Woodward took over his part with great success. In the next seventeen years the play was revived several times, chiefly at the instance of Woodward, who was, according to Davies, fond of the rôle of Parolles. Between 1763 and 1900 *All's Well* was acted only about once a decade. Among those who produced it in the nineteenth century were Samuel Phelps and Charles Fry. Most of the nineteenth century revivals made use of a bowdlerized version of the play arranged by Kemble.

The most recent English productions of *All's Well* were those of the Old Vic in London and of the Memorial Theater in Stratford-on-Avon, both in 1922. The same year saw a German production at the Schauspielhaus in Graz. Dr. E. Mühlbach lists, in the *Shakespeare-Jahrbuch* for 1921, eight German performances in the years 1911-1920. There seems to be no record of any American performance.

APPENDIX C

THE TEXT OF THE PRESENT EDITION

The text of the present edition is based, by permission of the Oxford University Press, upon that of the Oxford Shakespeare, edited by the late W. J. Craig, which has been collated with the Folio of 1623. The following deviations have been made from Craig's text:

1. The stage-directions are those of the Folio: additional directions, where necessary, have been printed within square brackets.

2. A number of minor changes in punctuation, not affecting the meaning of the passages involved, have been made without comment. The spelling of a few words has been normalized: e.g. warlike has been substituted for war-like, theoric for theorick, villainy for villany and wagon for waggon.

3. The forms 'y'are' and 'th'art,' where they occur in the Folio, have been restored in place of the 'you're' and 'thou'rt' of Craig's text. The Folio has also been followed in the use of such elisions as 'th' inaudible.'

4. The following changes of text have been made, in almost every instance in accord with the Folio. The readings of the present edition precede the colon: those of Craig follow it:

I. i.	62	to have—: have it.
	67	*Count.*: *Hel.*
	97	'Twere: It were
	116	Looks bleak i' th': Look bleak in the
	131	setting: sitting
	168	commodity will: commodity that will
	212	hath: have
ii.	56	This: Thus
	67	You're loved: You are lov'd
iii.	92	o'er: for
	179	loveliness: loneliness

257	an: and
II. i. 2	gain all,: gain, all (F)
23	Farewell. [*To another Lord.*] Come hither to me. [*They converse.*]: Farewell. Come hither to me. [*Exit attended.*
50	Stay the king.: Stay: the king. *Re-enter King; Parolles and Bertram retire.*
64	see: fee
68	I would I had, so: I would I had: so
93	wondering: wond'ring
94	[*He retires to the door.*]: [*Exit.*
96	*Laf.* [*to Helena without.*] Nay, come your ways. *Enter Helen.*: *Re-enter Lafeu with Helena. Laf.* Nay, come your ways.
147	sits (shifts F): fits
158	imposture (impostrue F): imposter
163	greatest: great'st
167	her: his
184	courage, all: courage, virtue, all
ii. 73	them?: them. (F)
75	me.: me?
iii. 11	*Par.* So I say—both of Galen and Paracelsus.: *Par.* So I say. *Laf.* Both of Galen and Paracelsus. *Par.* So I say.
24, 25	in What-do-you-call there. (in what do you call there F): in—what do you call there—.
33	he's: he is
34	facinerious: facinorous
39-44	*Laf.* In a most weak— *Par.* And debile . . . as to be— *Laf.* Generally thankful.: *Laf.* In a most weak and debile . . . as to be generally thankful.
60	sovereign: sov'reign
127	stands: stand
160	that: thou
215	burthen: burden
234	wiser—: wiser.
235	Ev'n: E'en
279	commission: heraldry
280	heraldry: commission
285	What's: What is
300	regions: regions!
308	Wars: War
iv. 17	fortune: fortunes
29	Away! [Before God,] th'art a knave.: Away! Thou'rt a knave.

57   *Par.* I shall report it so. *Exit Parolles.* *Hel.* [*to Clown.*] I pray you come, sirrah. *Exit* [*followed by Clown.*]: *Par.* I shall report it so. *Hel.* I pray you. Come, sirrah. [*Exeunt.*

v. 20   well, I, sir. He, sir's,: well. Ay sir; he, sir, is

27   at's: at his

95   [*To Clown.*] Where are my other men? [*To Parolles.*] Monsieur, farewell. *Exit.*: *Ber.* [*To Parolles.*] Where are my other men, monsieur? [*To Helena.*] Farewell. [*Exit Helena.*

III. ii. 9   hold: sold

14   lings: ling

108   none-sparing: non-sparing

113   still-pairing (still-peering F): still-piecing

iii. 7   prosperous: prosp'rous

iv. 15   dogs: dog

v. 25   threatens: threaten

51   Whatsome'er: Whatsoe'er

66   I write,: Ay, right;

vi. 39   ours: ore

66   stomach, to 't: stomach to 't

68   his: its

106   imbost: embossed

vii. 8, 17   count he: county

34   After,: After this,

IV. i. 15   E'en: Even

46   mule: mute

60   leapt: leaped

68   You shall: Thou shalt

71   *Cargo, cargo, cargo,*: *Cargo, cargo,*

ii. 24   high'st: Highest

25   Jove's: God's

36   recovers: recover

38   scarre: scarr

62   that, what in time proceeds,: that what in time proceeds

iii. 31   meant: most

66   makes: make

100   congied: conge'd

114   module: has: model; he has

199   Dumaine: Dumain (and so throughout)

297   he's: he is

300   has: he has

312	not to ask: not ask
v. 15	sallets: salads
18	sallet: salad
19	herbs: salad-herbs
42	fisnomy: phisnomy
68, 87	a': he
V. i. 26	seem: seems
iii. 31	sets: set
47	enfixing: infixing
60	rash: rasher
71	Which: *Count.* Which
96	ingag'd: engag'd
153	[*Exeunt some Attendants.*]: *Exeunt the gentle Astringer, and some Attendants.*
158	*Enter Widow, Diana and Parolles* [*with Attendants*].: *Re-enter the gentle Astringer, with Widow and Diana.*
166	count: county
197	hit: it
204	[*Exit Parolles covertly.*]: [omits]
255	He's: He is

even (adj.): **112** (V. iii. 331)
even (vb.): **13** (I. iii. 3)
event: **56** (III. ii. 107)
examin'd: **62** (III. v. 63)
exception: **11** (I. ii. 40)
excess: **3** (I. i. 68)
exempted: **30** (II. i. 198)
exorcist: **111** (V. iii. 309)
expecting: **41** (II. iii. 189)
expedient: **40** (II. iii. 186)
express'd: **102** (V. iii. 50)

facinerious: **35** (II. iii. 34)
faculties: **21** (I. iii. 234)
faith: **73** (IV. i. 82)
fall (noun): **23** (II. i. 13)
fall (vb.): **52** (III. i. 22)
falls: **97** (V. i. 37)
fated sky: **9** (I. i. 236)
fathers: **12** (I. ii. 62)
favour: **4** (I. i. 95)
fear: **61** (III. v. 30)
fee-simple: **88** (IV. iii. 314)
fellows: **34** (II. iii. 12)
fetch off: **65** (III. vi. 19)
figure: **52** (III. i. 12)
file: **58** (III. iii. 9)
fine (adj.): **110** (V. iii. 273)
fine (noun): **91** (IV. iv. 35)
fire: **70** (III. vii. 26)
fisnomy: **93** (IV. v. 42)
fistula: **2** (I. i. 40)
fit (adv.): **5** (I. i. 114)
fit (vb.): **26** (II. i. 93)
fleshes: **78** (IV. iii. 19)
flinch: **30** (II. i. 190)
Florence: **10** (I. ii. 12)
follow: **27** (II. i. 102)
fond: **15** (I. iii. 77)
for (because): **38** (II. iii. 131)
for (toward): **89** (IV. iii. 357)
for (worthy of): **68** (III. vi. 108)
foregoers: **39** (II. iii. 144)

forehorse: **24** (II. i. 30)
fore-past: **104** (V. iii. 121)
forfeited: **44** (II. iii. 284)
forged: **4** (I. i. 86)
forsake: **36** (II. iii. 62)
forward top: **101** (V. iii. 39)
found thee: **41** (II. iii. 215)
frames: **52** (III. i. 12)
frank: **11** (I. ii. 20)
from word to word: **69** (III. vii. 10)
fruitfully: **33** (II. ii. 75)
fry: **86** (IV. iii. 251)
furnish: **3** (I. i. 79)
furnish to: **45** (II. iii. 307)
furniture: **36** (II. iii. 65)

gait: **25** (II. i. 55)
gamester: **107** (V. iii. 190)
gather: **74** (IV. i. 87)
gave him out: **34** (II. iii. 14)
general: **21** (I. iii. 232)
generally: **1** (I. i. 8)
gentle: **96** (V. i. 6)
glass: **29** (II. i. 168)
go: **2** (I. i. 50)
go about: **20** (I. iii. 196)
go to the world: **14** (I. iii. 21)
go under: **60** (III. v. 21)
go with: **91** (IV. iv. 29)
goes upon: **96** (V. i. 13)
good proceeding: **109** (V. iii. 238)
good sadness: **85** (IV. iii. 230)
gossips: **7** (I. i. 191)
grace (noun): **99** (V. ii. 51)
grace (vb.): **4** (I. i. 92); **66** (III. vi. 70)
great: **2** (I. i. 31)
great way: **5** (I. i. 113)
gross: **19** (I. iii. 180)
grossly: **19** (I. iii. 186)
grounds: **69** (III. vii. 3)

motion (movement): **42** (II. iii. 246)

motions: **110** (V. iii. 267)

motive: **91** (IV. iv. 20)

mounts: **9** (I. i. 239)

move: **10** (I. ii. 6)

muffled: **74** (IV. i. 95)

multiplying medicine: **104** (V. iii. 102)

muse: **50** (II. v. 71)

must: **8** (I. i. 201)

muster: **25** (II. i. 55)

mystery: **66** (III. vi. 67)

native: **9** (I. i. 242); **18** (I. iii. 154)

naturalize: **9** (I. i. 227)

nature (manner): **84** (IV. iii. 176)

nature (life): **87** (IV. iii. 274)

naughty: **110** (V. iii. 256)

nearest: **81** (IV. iii. 101)

necessitied to: **103** (V. iii. 85)

need: **50** (II. v. 73)

Nessus: **87** (IV. iii. 283)

next: **15** (I. iii. 64)

nice: **96** (V. i. 15)

no: **5** (I. i. 120)

noble: **33** (II. ii. 66)

nobler: **40** (II. iii. 178)

noise: **45** (II. iii. 314)

no other: **19** (I. iii. 173); **65** (III. vi. 26)

nose-herbs: **92** (IV. v. 20)

not: **7** (I. i. 181)

note (attention): **64** (III. v. 101)

note (fame): **18** (I. iii. 165)

note (writing): **21** (I. iii. 235)

notes: **21** (I. iii. 234)

nothing (adv.): **69** (III. vii. 5)

nothing (noun): **26** (II. i. 95)

novices: **25** (II. i. 48)

now-born brief: **40** (II. iii. 186)

numbered: **94** (IV. v. 87)

obedient right: **40** (II. iii. 167)

observance: **53** (III. ii. 5)

occasions: **96** (V. i. 14)

o'er: **16** (I. iii. 92)

o'erflows: **79** (IV. iii. 30)

of (in respect of): **38** (II. iii. 126)

of (partner in): **79** (IV. iii. 55)

of (some of): **49** (II. v. 51)

offic'd: **57** (III. ii. 129)

on 't: **18** (I. iii. 144)

one: **4** (I. i. 97)

ordinaries: **41** (II. iii. 210)

our own: **78** (IV. iii. 25)

out: **12** (I. ii. 58)

out of act: **11** (I. ii. 30)

out with 't: **6** (I. i. 161)

outward: **52** (III. i. 11)

overlooking: **2** (I. i. 46)

over-night: **59** (III. iv. 23)

owes: **23** (II. i. 9)

pace: **94** (IV. v. 71)

parcel: **36** (II. iii. 58)

parcels: **81** (IV. iii. 104)

part: **10** (I. ii. 15); **77** (IV. ii. 50)

particular (detail): **85** (IV. iii. 207)

particular (individual): **4** (I. i. 98)

particular (part): **50** (II. v. 67)

parting: **49** (II. v. 62)

pass: **49** (II. v. 59)

passage: **2** (I. i. 21)

past: **28** (II. i. 127)

patent: **94** (IV. v. 70)

pen down: **67** (III. vi. 79)

perfect: **90** (IV. iv. 4)

rush: **32** (II. ii. 25)
ruttish: **86** (IV. iii. 243)

sadness: **85** (IV. iii. 230)
saffron: **92** (IV. v. 2)
Saint Jaques' pilgrim: **58** (III. iv. 4)
sallets: **92** (IV. v. 15)
sanctified: **6** (I. i. 154)
sanctify: **5** (I. i. 110); **58** (III. iv. 11)
satisfaction: **103** (V. iii. 100)
scarre: **76** (IV. ii. 38)
science: **104** (V. iii. 103)
scores: **86** (IV. iii. 254)
season: **101** (V. iii. 32)
self-gracious: **94** (IV. v. 79)
self-unable: **52** (III. i. 13)
Senoys: **10** (I. ii. 1)
sense (faculty): **17** (I. iii. 116); **35** (II. iii. 54); **59** (III. iv. 39)
sense (reason): **9** (I. i. 244); **28** (II. i. 127)
sequent: **33** (II. ii. 60)
servants: **4** (I. i. 86)
serve: **10** (I. ii. 15)
service: **11** (I. ii. 27)
setting down: **5** (I. i. 131)
set up against: **2** (I. i. 36)
set up your rest: **28** (II. i. 138)
several: **13** (I. ii. 74)
shall: **81** (IV. iii. 93)
shallow: **14** (I. iii. 46)
shameful hate: **102** (V. iii. 66)
share with: **3** (I. i. 74)
sharp: **96** (V. i. 14)
should: **75** (IV. ii. 11)
show: **18** (I. iii. 140)
showing: **34** (II. iii. 24)
shows (noun): **28** (II. i. 153)
shows (vb.): **60** (III. v. 23)
shrewd (evil): **62** (III. v. 68)

shrewd (sharp-tongued): **94** (IV. v. 67)
shrewdly (keenly): **63** (III. v. 89)
shrewdly (vilely): **109** (V. iii. 234)
shrieve's fool: **85** (IV. iii. 213)
shut up: **8** (I. i. 199)
simpleness: **3** (I. i. 52)
sit: **5** (I. i. 114)
sith: **106** (V. iii. 156)
sithence: **17** (I. iii. 126)
slip: **18** (I. iii. 154)
smack: **42** (II. iii. 236)
smock: **24** (II. i. 30)
smoked: **68** (III. vi. 110)
snipt-taffeta: **92** (IV. v. 2)
snuff: **12** (I. ii. 59)
so: **39** (II. iii. 186)
solely: **5** (I. i. 113)
sovereignty: **21** (I. iii. 232)
space: **74** (IV. i. 93)
spacious: **25** (II. i. 51)
special (extraordinary): **31** (II. ii. 7)
special (particular): **26** (II. i. 95)
speed: **66** (III. vi. 71)
spend: **96** (V. i. 8)
sphere: **4** (I. i. 101)
spoil: **78** (IV. iii. 20)
sprat: **68** (III. vi. 112)
square: **28** (II. i. 153)
staggers: **40** (II. iii. 170)
stain: **5** (I. i. 123)
staining act: **69** (III. vii. 7)
stall: **17** (I. iii. 133)
stand: **6** (I. i. 147); **10** (I. ii. 15)
stands off: **38** (II. iii. 127)
start: **54** (III. ii. 52)
starts: **109** (V. iii. 234)
stay: **25** (II. i. 50)
stay upon: **61** (III. v. 45)
steads: **70** (III. vii. 41)
steal: **67** (III. vi. 97)